A powerful read that transforms educational mindsets, captivates the heart, and meets readers where they are in understanding and using liberatory practices. The authors offer compelling research, practical strategies, and inspirations for holistic approaches to stress-wise wellness, including race-equity-based frameworks, class discussions, and developmentally responsive exercises. Do not bother putting it on your shelf; leave it on your desk or a place you frequent because this is a resource you will turn to again and again for planned or in-the-moment inspiration, grounding, and impact. Bringing to the forefront what we should all embrace for the health, wellness, and resilience of students and ourselves as educators and school leaders.

—**Senta Greene**, MA, CCLS, leading expert in educational reform and diversity, equity, and inclusion strategist, Full Circle Consulting Systems, Inc.

Stress and mental health are both invisible forces that shape every school and classroom. While we understand the impact of stress on learning and classroom dynamics, there are simply too few resources to support teachers with practices that can foster well-being. *From Stressed Out to Stress Wise* offers a brilliant pathway for classrooms and schools to transform how educators and students connect and learn. The stress-wise approach in this book offers readers profound insights and useful practices that cultivate the joy, belonging, and well-being we all need and deserve. This book is a must-read for teachers, educators, and practitioners searching for a fresh and deeply authentic model for transforming classrooms and schools.

—**Shawn Ginwright**, PhD, Jerome T. Murphy Professor of the Practice Chair, Harvard Graduate School of Education, and Chief Executive Officer, Flourish Agenda, Oakland, CA

Stress is inevitable. This book doesn't argue with that, but rather lights the way for us to skillfully be with what is. *From Stressed Out to Stress Wise* isn't simply a powerful educational resource—it's a treasure trove of practices that take working with stress out of the realm of theory, grounding it in the everyday classroom. This book is practical and transformative. *From Stressed Out to Stress Wise* belongs in the hands of everyone working with youth!

—**Caverly Morgan**, founder of Peace in Schools and author of *A Kids Book About Mindfulness* and *The Heart of Who We Are: Realizing Freedom Together*

*From Stressed Out to Stress Wise* is a timely, accessible, and essential guide for educators that has the potential to not only enhance student flourishing, but impact the well-being of the entire ecosystem of a classroom and beyond. Beautifully grounded in holistic, indigenous wisdom traditions as well as evidence-based approaches for supporting social-emotional learning, this book is full of practical applications, heartfelt practices, and insightful explorations that support self-care and collective caring. It provides an elegant framework for honoring the complexities of guiding young learners in their wholeness.

—**Rashmi S. Bismark**, MD, MPH, preventive medicine consultant, mindfulness and yoga educator, and author of *Finding Om* (illustrated by Morgan Huff)

Rising rates of depression, anxiety disorders, and self-injurious behavior attest to the harmful levels of stress experienced by today's students. Wills, Deva, and Saccareccia's accessible and captivating new book provides educators with a detailed roadmap for cultivating in their students stress awareness and a trove of self-regulation skills to manage stress, informed by yogic, mindfulness, and compassion-based approaches. The authors' clear, engaging content, powerful metaphors, and multiple options for implementation will position educators to equip students with the long-neglected wellness and stress-management skills so sorely needed in our schools.

—**Drew Erhardt**, PhD, professor, Pepperdine University, Graduate School of Education & Psychology

## Praise for *From Stressed Out to Stress Wise: How You and Your Students Can Navigate Challenges and Nurture Vitality*

This book is a powerful combination of grounded scholarship, practical methods, and heartfelt advocacy for both teachers and students. It contains engaging case examples, excellent summaries on the science of stress, and clear descriptions of what teachers and students need to thrive in the classroom and in their lives.

—**David Treleaven**, PhD, author of *Trauma-Sensitive Mindfulness: Practices for Safe and Transformative Healing*

A beautiful, straightforward guide to helping young people and those who love them to coregulate their way to mindful resilience. Widely inclusive in its explanation of often invisible stressors on all nervous systems, the wisdom in this book is both timeless and up-to-the minute in terms of its understanding of physiology, neuroscience, and strategies for addressing society's biggest challenges, starting with our students.

—**Dr. Chris Willard**, author of *Alphabreaths* and faculty at Harvard Medical School

*From Stressed Out to Stress Wise* is simply the best book I have seen on the market for middle school classrooms. The collective wisdom of Wills, Deva, and Saccareccia will no doubt become the benchmark for social and emotional learning. Clearly, they are experts in communicating with middle schoolers and those who teach them. I highly recommend this book.

—**Joanne Spence**, MA, author of *Trauma-Informed Yoga: A Toolbox for Therapists: 47 Practices to Calm, Balance, and Restore the Nervous System* and executive director of Yoga in Schools

*From Stressed Out to Stress Wise* condenses years of classroom experience into a thoughtful, usable, powerful guide to growing embodied wellness, belonging, and sustainability in yourself, your students, your school, and your community. This masterfully sequenced, multifaceted exploration of stress engages teens in cultivating greater awareness, social-emotional intelligence, compassion, and competence such that they can successfully navigate a stress-filled world by making wise choices for themselves.

—**Leah Kalish**, MA, ERYT, ECYT, Family Constellation & Embodiment Process

The authors' extensive experience working with children and in schools is evident on every page of this excellent book. Practical yet impactful advice is coupled with accessible methods to help teachers and administrators embody wisdom and compassion and infuse it into their school culture.

—**Susan Kaiser Greenland**, author of *The Mindful Child* and *Mindful Games* and cofounder of Inner Kids

An incredibly timely and constructive book that will have a positive impact on the social-emotional growth of young learners. As we become more cognizant of the effects stress has on our mental, physical, and emotional health, we can either let stress paralyze and defeat us or harness its energy and use it to our advantage. Each chapter in this book provides valuable tools and examples to help educators guide young learners in becoming more aware of their emotional reactions to stress. "Stress-wise" learners will take this skillset into adulthood. I can only envision a world where, as adults, they will continue to employ these abilities in their daily lives as models of social and emotional balance.

—**Jasmin Saidi-Kuehnert**, MBA, founder, president, and CEO, Academic Credentials Evaluation Institute, Inc. (ACEI)

This is the book that educators, administrators, and parents need to read and experience. It combines theory, science, and many new paradigms for managing stress that I have never seen before in 25 years of teaching. This book is revolutionary in that it combines ancient wisdom with modern methods when becoming wise to stress. There is a breadth and depth to this book that allows for deep digestion of the material while still keeping the language simple and implementable. The authors have spent time on the ground in the classroom, and it shows.

—**Amy Wheeler**, past president of the International Association of Yoga Therapists and founder of Optimal State

What an exciting approach to helping students and teachers engage in lifelong practices to positively identify and manage the many stressors of daily life. The authors share not only a framework but also specific strategies, activities, and classroom examples in clear, manageable segments, making effective implementation imminently doable. I highly recommend this book to all educators who want to transform their classroom daily practices to build vitality, balance, and caring relationships for themselves and their students.

—**Dr. Patrice Pujol**, retired teacher, principal, and school superintendent

# From STRESSED OUT to STRESS WISE

# From STRESSED OUT to STRESS WISE

How You and Your Students Can Navigate Challenges and Nurture Vitality

Abby Wills | Anjali Deva | Niki Saccareccia

Arlington, Virginia USA

2800 Shirlington Road, Suite 1001 • Arlington, VA 22206 USA
Phone: 800-933-2723 or 703-578-9600 • Fax: 703-575-5400
Website: www.ascd.org • Email: member@ascd.org
Author guidelines: www.ascd.org/write

Richard Culatta, *Chief Executive Officer;* Anthony Rebora, *Chief Content Officer;* Genny Ostertag, *Managing Director, Book Acquisitions & Editing;* Susan Hills, *Senior Acquisitions Editor;* Mary Beth Nielsen, *Director, Book Editing;* Miriam Calderone, *Editor;* Thomas Lytle, *Creative Director;* Donald Ely, *Art Director;* Lindsey Smith/The Hatcher Group and Lisa Hill, *Graphic Designers;* Cynthia Stock, *Typesetter;* Kelly Marshall, *Production Manager;* Shajuan Martin, *E-Publishing Specialist*

Copyright © 2023 ASCD. All rights reserved. It is illegal to reproduce copies of this work in print or electronic format (including reproductions displayed on a secure intranet or stored in a retrieval system or other electronic storage device from which copies can be made or displayed) without the prior written permission of the publisher. By purchasing only authorized electronic or print editions and not participating in or encouraging piracy of copyrighted materials, you support the rights of authors and publishers. Readers who wish to reproduce or republish excerpts of this work in print or electronic format may do so for a small fee by contacting the Copyright Clearance Center (CCC), 222 Rosewood Dr., Danvers, MA 01923, USA (phone: 978-750-8400; fax: 978-646-8600; web: www.copyright.com). To inquire about site licensing options or any other reuse, contact ASCD Permissions at www.ascd.org/permissions or permissions@ascd.org. For a list of vendors authorized to license ASCD e-books to institutions, see www.ascd.org/epubs. Send translation inquiries to translations@ascd.org.

ASCD® is a registered trademark of Association for Supervision and Curriculum Development. All other trademarks contained in this book are the property of, and reserved by, their respective owners, and are used for editorial and informational purposes only. No such use should be construed to imply sponsorship or endorsement of the book by the respective owners.

All web links in this book are correct as of the publication date below but may have become inactive or otherwise modified since that time. If you notice a deactivated or changed link, please email books@ascd.org with the words "Link Update" in the subject line. In your message, please specify the web link, the book title, and the page number on which the link appears.

PAPERBACK ISBN: 978-1-4166-3216-0   ASCD product #123004                     n7/23
PDF EBOOK ISBN: 978-1-4166-3217-7; see Books in Print for other formats.

Quantity discounts are available: email programteam@ascd.org or call 800-933-2723, ext. 5773, or 703-575-5773. For desk copies, go to www.ascd.org/deskcopy.

**Library of Congress Cataloging-in-Publication Data**

Names: Wills, Abby, author. | Deva, Anjali, author. | Saccareccia, Niki, author.
 Title: From stressed out to stress wise : how you and your students can navigate challenges and nurture vitality / Abby Wills, Anjali Deva, and  Niki Saccareccia.
Description: Arlington, VA : ASCD, [2023] | Includes bibliographical references and index.
Identifiers: LCCN 2023007797 (print) | LCCN 2023007798 (ebook) | ISBN 9781416632160 (paperback) | ISBN 9781416632177 (pdf)
Subjects: LCSH: Classroom environment—Psychological aspects—United States. | Stress management. | Mindfulness (Psychology) | Team learning approach in education—United States. | Middle school teaching—United States. | High school teaching—United States.
Classification: LCC LB3013 .W543 2023 (print) | LCC LB3013 (ebook) | DDC 370.15/8—dc23/eng/20230315
LC record available at https://lccn.loc.gov/2023007797
LC ebook record available at https://lccn.loc.gov/2023007798

---

32 31 30 29 28 27 26 25 24 23           1 2 3 4 5 6 7 8 9 10 11 12

Abby
~
*For each and every student.*

Anjali
~
*This work is dedicated to any human being willing to lean in, turn toward themselves, and take a look within. The courage and bravery it takes to grow is a practice of becoming stress wise and a process we are honored to co-create with you.*

Niki
~
*To every educator, ally, and advocate helping to make the cultural shift in education—to one that nourishes all aspects of our humanness in the learning environment, including the strategic importance of rest and reflection—not only possible but realized.*

# From STRESSED OUT to STRESS WISE

How You and Your Students Can Navigate Challenges and Nurture Vitality

Acknowledgments ................................................................................. xiii

1. Becoming Stress Wise ........................................................................ 1

2. Know: Exploring Stress and Vitality in the Classroom Through the Scope of Awareness ............................................. 22

3. Differentiate: The Science of Stress ............................................. 48

4. Identify: Sources of Stress, Coping, and Vitality ....................... 73

5. Discern: Making Wise Choices ..................................................... 92

6. Resource: Building a Healthy Relationship with Stress ........ 115

7. Relate: A Stress-Wise Classroom Culture ................................. 154

Bibliography ......................................................................................... 178

Index ...................................................................................................... 183

About the Authors .............................................................................. 188

# Acknowledgments

## Abby

I am deeply grateful for the many individuals and institutions that have supported my development as an educator, contemplative practitioner, and writer. To my coauthors, Anjali Deva and Niki Saccareccia: thank you for enthusiastically joining this project and contributing your expertise. This work would not be possible without the courage and trust of the thousands of students who have willingly participated in my courses over the past two decades in schools. I am indebted to their brilliance and wisdom. Patrice Pujol, John Riley, and Jeanne Weierheiser, thank you all for encouraging me to write. Tremendous respect to my many teachers and mentors, too many to name, including Senta Greene, Leah Kalish, Tsoknyi Rinpoche, Dr. Angel Acosta, Olga Winbush, Rebecca Trujillo Vest, Shelah Lehrer-Graiwer, and Gloria Walther. Gratitude to the schools and organizations that have provided the fields for this work to grow. Gigantic love to my Ma, Aaron Wills, Falken, and Clay, for your patience and understanding as I pour my heart into my work.

To our editors at ASCD, Susan Hills and Miriam Calderone, your guidance has been invaluable.

## Anjali

I am so grateful for the opportunity to work with and learn from my coauthors, Abby and Niki, on this project. My contributions here are guided by the wisdom of my ancestors, lineage, and the tradition of Ayurveda and yoga. This work is a reflection of the knowledge and wisdom handed down to me by my father, Arun Deva, without whom none of this would have been possible. My mother, Meeta Deva, is the reason I choose to do the work that I do. Her bright and courageous spirit live on in me, and I hope to honor her by sharing in this way. My utmost gratitude to all my students and clients over the years who have shown up with curiosity, dedication, and a willingness to step outside of the box; it would not have been possible without you. To my family, Alex, Danger, and Stella: thank you for your love, patience, and encouragement.

## Niki

I must acknowledge my coauthors, Abby and Anjali, for their expertise and grace as we worked on this project together. To my grandmother, Parvaneh Bahar, and her lifetime dedication in making the world a kinder and more educated place by advocating for others whose voices were difficult to hear. To my dear friends, parents, and colleagues for their confidence and encouragement. To my partner, Matt, for his unyielding support and love. I am indebted to my own teachers who have shared their knowledge and lived experience so that I can stand on their shoulders and do the same: Maria Cristina Jiminez, Gil Hedley, Leslie Kaminoff, Jill Miller, and Sri Sri Ravi Shankar. And to my students and clients who give me their trust to share these powerful practices and stand firmly rooted in the yogic path.

# 1

# Becoming Stress Wise

*Our job as educators isn't just to teach.*
*Our job is to show up fully human.*

—Dr. Shawn Ginwright

What first comes to mind when you think about stress in your classroom? Does it impede the learning process for students or interfere with your ability to teach? Our mindsets around stress are often influenced by stress itself—we may view it as the inevitable by-product of a hurried life or as the fuel that helps us "get the job done." But what if stress is actually a signal for change, relaying a message from a deeper source of wisdom?

Stress is part of an elegant biological process that protects us from threat. It only becomes a problem when we ignore the wise signals our bodies generate in response to stimuli. When we keep pushing forward despite our bodies experiencing distress—be it in the form of impossible workloads, social pressures, inadequate emotional support, or even lack of sleep—we end up in a vicious cycle that depletes our energies.

Stress affects every aspect of school life—academics, social interactions, emotional development—for both teachers and students. Left unchecked, unresolved distress can lead to a host of physical, mental, and social ills (Liu et al., 2017). It's common for us to get stuck in reactionary patterns that keep unhealthy conditions in place. Instead, we need to develop specific skills to realize the synergy between stress and vitality. In the right dose and environment, stress can promote creativity, compassion, innovation, and resilience. The right environment can mean either the psychobiological environment of our bodies or the social environment of our classroom, school, or home. Listening to the signals of stress can show us what needs to change in our lives.

In our view, stress and vitality are not binary but, rather, exist on a spectrum, and our well-being depends on our ability to navigate between them. Those with a high "stress intelligence" or "stress IQ" leverage stress to empower them rather than letting it shame or deplete them. To be "stress wise" is to cultivate lifelong habits, mindsets, skills, and ways of being that optimize learning, cognitive development, and community building. The purpose of this book is to help you create a classroom of stress-wise learners who can maintain their well-being while modulating stressors and engaging in sustainable learning.

How might our time in school be different if we develop habits that move us closer to vitality—habits like slowing down to be more aware of our experiences and investigating stressors rather than immediately reacting to them? Is it possible to make choices that serve the collective well-being of those in the classroom rather than relying on short-term solutions to cope? Getting wise about stress is a lifelong, life-affirming process that starts with discovering how different kinds of stress function in our lives. With practice, we can recognize whether stress is motivating or depleting us and how to respond to it mindfully.

## Stress IQ

Stress IQ is the ability to accept stress as an aspect of well-being and to modulate our responses to it to sustain vitality. This requires us to be increasingly aware of the sources and impact of stress and to practice physiological and emotional coregulation. By developing our stress IQ, we allow innate human wisdom to emerge and flourish in the face of life's inevitable stressors. Stress-wise learners, educators, and caregivers harness positive stress for creativity, navigate tolerable stress through appropriate resourcing, and proactively heal the effects of toxic stress.

## Stress IQ as Integral to a Healthy Classroom

Any educational endeavor that does not include the well-being of the learner as a core consideration may do more harm than good. After all, what good is a 4.0 GPA if achieving it results in life-threatening depression? Bettina Love (2019) says it best: "If students are not well, test scores do not matter" (p. 160). Test scores will improve when students know that they themselves matter and when school leaders center healing, especially in cases where institutional and racial power dynamics are contributing to students' trauma.

Exploring stress can increase our social awareness. In the stress-wise classroom, the group is aware of itself as a collective entity. Care and compassion emerge more readily when the group is aware and nimble enough to recognize, respond to, and coregulate stress in times of grief and challenge. Given the effects of peer pressure and profound shifts in brain development during the school years, fostering stress IQ alongside emotional IQ has far-reaching implications for students' self-esteem and a sense of belonging. Our ability to cope with stress is directly affected by our self-efficacy (e.g., "I don't know how I will get through this, but I can try" versus "There's no way I can deal with this").

As students become more self-aware, more compassionate, and more regularly resourced (that is, consistently accessing and using resources to navigate stress), their self-efficacy also changes. Collective stress IQ is the result of cultivating well-being in service to a vision of social transformation and justice. When we focus solely on our individual survival, inequities abound, but when we become skilled in attuning to one another, we are better able to see and care for one another's needs.

## Stress IQ Within the System

We want to be clear that the responsibility for change does not lie with individual students or educators alone. Though stress IQ is hardly the *only* factor in maintaining a healthy classroom, it *is* critical, and it includes a host of key cofactors. Stress intelligence acknowledges the macrosystemic forces that interrupt our well-being. Speaking on the podcast *Hurry Slowly,* Nkem Ndefo (Ndefo & Glei, 2021) speaks to this dynamic:

> I've yet to meet a system that changed itself. Systems don't change themselves. People change systems. Typically, the people receiving the brunt of a system are tasked with changing it, not the people privileged by that system or receiving the gains in the system. So, while I reject individual narratives of resilience like "pull yourself up by your bootstraps," I do realize that those of us who are being punished by these systems do need more resilience so that we have the capacity and the space to do the healing internally and for our systems so that they do not inflict on us as they have historically.

Investigating how stress and vitality function within a group is key to developing collective stress IQ and prevents individuals from feeling undue pressure to manage stress that originates beyond the classroom. Our individual beliefs and behaviors affect the whole just as the beliefs and behaviors of the whole affect us. We acknowledge the disparate levels of health, efficacy, and corruption that permeate the systems in which we live and work. Although stress-wise strategies are intended for use in the classroom, the stress itself is rooted in a variety of systems—economic, judicial, agricultural, and more. Our stress-wise approach is not meant to bypass systemic injustice in any way but, rather, to help sustain efforts toward human thriving.

## Overview of Stress-Wise Praxis

We approach the work of stress regulation as a praxis rather than a linear or prescriptive curriculum. Praxis synthesizes theory, practice, and reflection in pursuit of practical applications, or actions, to carry out students' learning. Stress-wise praxis (see Figure 1.1) centers on adapting our responses to the demands of daily life in a way that enhances vitality and cultivates wisdom. Related practices integrate the physical, mental, and emotional domains of the individual as well as integrating the individual with the collective:

- **Physical or body-based practices** include simple postures, breathing exercises, and relaxation techniques that promote body awareness and nervous system regulation.

- **Mental or mind-based practices** include sensory and emotional awareness techniques that promote mindfulness by fostering individuals' present-moment awareness of themselves and the group.
- **Emotional or heart-based practices** promote compassion and self-compassion, attend to the personal and collective experience of suffering, and nurture community connection.

The body-mind-heart integrating practices in this book are derived from Indigenous wisdom traditions and contemplative modalities including yoga, mindfulness, somatics, and embodiment techniques. The overarching goals that each of these modalities has in common are to cultivate awareness, grow connection, and increase freedom, personally and collectively. Figure 1.1 offers a visual model of the elements of stress-wise practice.

Figure 1.1. Stress-Wise Praxis at a Glance

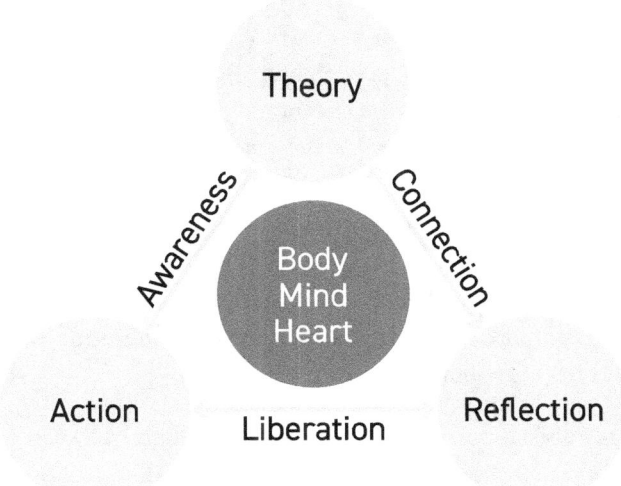

## Stress-Wise Praxis and Ayurveda

Stress-wise praxis is informed by Ayurveda, a traditional medical system from India. Ayurveda posits that food, sleep, and energy regulation are the three pillars of health. Anjali's clinical experience as an Ayurvedic practitioner over the last decade has taught her that individuals require unique combinations of these three factors to thrive. Just as different plants in a garden need varying amounts of sunlight, nitrogen, and water, different human beings require varying amounts of rest, exercise, and stress-reduction practices to flourish (Lad, 2012). Though plants in a garden must overcome stressors such as pests or drought, some stressors are necessary for them to grow—and the same is true for humans.

In the following chapters, we help you better understand the unique needs of your and your students' "gardens." Remembering that we are a part of nature helps us to sustain the ecosystems of which we are a part. Our classrooms, our families, our societies, and our world are all improved by our aware and compassionate presence within them.

## The Six-Mode Stress-Wise Framework

We developed the stress-wise framework for enhancing stress IQ over decades of work with students and educators:

- Abby's work with middle and high school students has helped shape the sequence of the modes in the framework. Over time, she has seen how this step-by-step approach helps students gain a deeper awareness of themselves and one another.
- Niki's background in Applied Behavior Analysis and her work as a mindfulness educator informs the framework's concise and pragmatic approach to unlearning and relearning ways of thinking and behaving.
- Anjali's clinical experience with Ayurveda and yoga offers a grounded understanding of how traditional wisdom systems may help each of us become more embodied and resilient.

The six-mode stress-wise framework (see Figure 1.2) can be applied to individuals, classrooms, and whole systems alike. Its purpose is to support stress modulation by ensuring that we

1. **Know** the physical, mental, emotional, and social signals of stress and vitality.
2. **Differentiate** between stress and distress.
3. **Identify** the origins of stress and vitality.

4. **Discern** appropriate methods of modulating stress and increasing vitality.
5. **Resource** our systems with practices for well-being.
6. **Relate** with peers and community to enact changes that support collective well-being.

Figure 1.2. Six-Mode Stress-Wise Framework

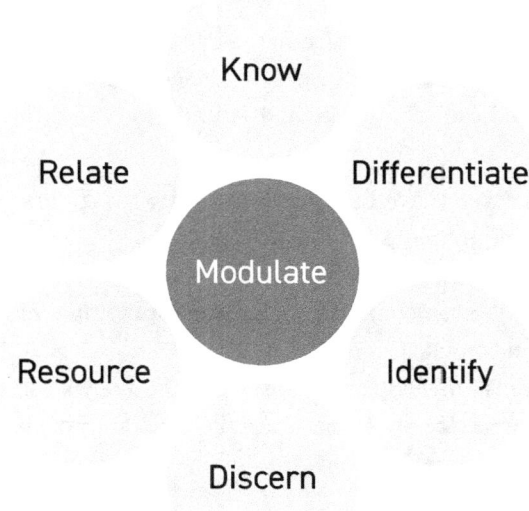

The chapters of this book are organized according to these six modes. Each chapter covers the purpose and function of each mode and provides supportive research and illustrative stories from the field, student surveys, educator reflections, and suggestions for carrying the practices forward. Each chapter also includes inquiry-based learning cycles (LCs) that include relational and personal stress-wise activities. There are five phases for each LC:

1. **Engage:** Students share what they already know about topics.
2. **Explore:** Students delve into interpersonal research of their lived experiences.
3. **Embody:** Students employ body-mind-heart practices.

4. **Expand:** Educators present new material to broaden and deepen student knowledge.
5. **Express:** Students reflect on their process and share their learning.

Learning cycles offer opportunities for you and your students to become researchers of your own well-being by cultivating stress IQ through a systematic process of investigation and discovery. Unlike in traditional educational processes, teachers take on a facilitator's role in the stress-wise framework, thus relieving them of having to know the answer to every question. Answers will emerge in partnership with students.

Stress-wise praxis is built upon a pedagogical bedrock informed by multiple domains of education, body-mind-heart well-being, and social change. It is

- **Constructivist:** We build knowledge and make meaning together through inquiry.
- **Contemplative:** We learn from our lived experiences.
- **Critical:** We see connections between individual experiences and social conditions.
- **Somatic:** We develop awareness of our body's wise messages.
- **Transformational:** We embrace the constancy of change.
- **Healing-centered:** We act to alleviate suffering and increase liberation.

# Stress Intelligence and Human Connection

This book is about your and your students' shared experience of stress, vitality, and well-being in the classroom. The act of learning is intimately connected to our internal worlds. Stress is a doorway not only to stress intelligence but also to establishing greater well-being in our lives. The practices suggested in this book are designed to guide middle and high school students through their inner experiences and increase their awareness of how they interact with the outer world; to be stress wise is to be self-aware. Though we are all different, none of us is truly separate. We have individual lives *and* we are inextricably connected (Birdsong,

2020). This interconnection is key to stress intelligence, which grows within a community.

In this book, we share examples of ways the stress-wise approach has worked to decrease harm and nurture community in classrooms and throughout schools. You will hear how students' lives have been transformed by a growing awareness of their ability to find inner balance—not as an act of compliance, but as an act of empowerment that extends beyond school walls. Most important, we invite you to reflect on how best to integrate this work into your own classroom culture.

We've heard countless times how effective the stress-wise model is at helping people feel more connected to themselves, to one another, to the planet, and to life itself. We've seen classrooms and schools become safer spaces where students and educators feel a deeper sense of joy, harmony, and satisfaction thanks to stress-wise praxis.

Abby recalls a particular middle school classroom where students regularly engaged in stress-wise practices. During an observation, the teacher led students through a brief grounding practice—a few minutes of movement connected to breath—and then invited them to share with one another how their weeks were going. Students shared a mix of feelings: "It's going good," "Pretty good, but I'm tired," "Not that great."

One student, Jordan, really didn't want to share a response, but a classmate encouraged him, so he reluctantly shared that he was having a "hell week." The teacher asked if he would like to say why. He said he was being bullied at lunch and couldn't handle it anymore. Another student, Ximena, said she saw this happen. Jordan got very upset, tears bursting from his eyes. "Why didn't you tell your friend to leave me alone?" he exclaimed. A close friend of Jordan went over to sit near him. The teacher led the class through a dialogue on the details of the situation. Students created a plan for how they were going to support Jordan at lunch so he would no longer feel alone. A small group of students who were friends with the student who had bullied Jordan considered ways to tell her they wouldn't stand for the bullying any longer.

Jordan's classmates let him know they would create a system of care for him. This is the kind of care and connection we see in classrooms where students are encouraged to serve as resources for personal and collective well-being. Students in such classrooms are willing to be vulnerable and share their real experiences because they trust one another. They are also inclined to extend their connections and mutuality outside the classroom. One student shared with us that stress-wise practices created connections with classmates that carried outside school and across the years. "Once you are able to be relaxed with someone," this student said, "once you've shared that experience of feeling like you can just be yourself, you have that special bond with that person forever." It is in this spirit of common humanity that we offer this work.

We envision a future where schools are sites not only of learning, but also of healing and liberation—and we want to wholeheartedly welcome you to this exploration. Understanding the sources and impact of stress in our lives and how to thrive through challenges is part of the journey toward realizing this vision. Thank you for the important work you do and for allowing us to support your efforts.

# How to Use This Book

*Time and memory are true artists;*
*they remold reality nearer to the heart's desire.*

—John Dewey

Finding time to equip students with the skills they need to effectively deal with stress can be tricky, but if we're going to commit to nurturing students' well-being, find it we must. After all, any time we spend helping students develop stress intelligence will free up time in the long run by making them more accountable for their own decisions. We have found that students with high stress IQ are better equipped than others to manage their time, navigate challenges, and have meaningful and productive interactions. We hope this will be your experience as well.

At what time of the day or week do you feel most balanced and able to attend to students' social-emotional development? What part of your curricular schedule is most flexible? The answers to these questions offer clues for implementing the stress-wise framework, which consists of 23 learning cycles of 5 phases each. Full LCs range from 60 to 100 minutes long, and each phase within an LC is 5 to 20 minutes long (though we suggest carving out 20 minutes per phase over time). Here are a few options for implementation:

- **Steady plan:** 40–60 minutes per week, all at once or split into two or three 20-minute sessions. Each LC spans two weeks, with a new LC introduced every other week. To complete all LCs in this plan in one school year, use the minimum times given for each phase and occasionally combine phases.
- **Concentrated plan:** 90 minutes per week, presented as a single block or divided into 20- to 30-minute sessions. This plan allows for one LC to be completed per week.
- **Immersive plan:** Up to 90 minutes per day over 23 days at any frequency per week. All LCs can be completed within this time frame.
- **Make-it-your-own plan:** You decide how much time to devote to the framework each day or week and which phases of the LCs will benefit your students most.

Integrating the framework into your classroom will become increasingly fluid as you and your students become more familiar with it. We encourage you to allow ample time for meaningful engagement even if it means you do not complete all LCs within a school year.

# Essential Delineations

The stress-wise model deviates significantly from standard educational paradigms focused on standardization, memorization, and the gamification of academic success through popularity, accolades, and high scores. Schools that embrace stress-wise praxis must tolerate and even invite disruptions to the status quo. The metrics for successfully raising a stress-wise student body are open-ended, not dependent on goals, and, in many cases, disorienting (at first). Following are some ways in which our model differs from conventional approaches to education.

## Potential Outcomes Versus Traditional Outcomes

Some outcomes of developing a stress IQ are immeasurable because they reflect lifelong processes. In fact, as we write this book, we're still developing our own stress IQs. You'll know stress-wise praxis is at work in your classroom when more conversations open up around challenges and when students feel better able to access resources; when there is more connection, less conflict, more resilience, less disengagement, more creativity, and less rote memorization.

## Cultural Shifts Versus Quick Fixes

Well-being grows best when there is a stable, long-term commitment to it. The stress-wise model can be integrated over time in whatever ways work best for you and your students. Give yourself time to find your footing. Trust your own experience and common sense when considering how to respond to stress in your classroom. No one knows your students like you do, and no one knows their individual experiences like they do.

## Liberation Versus Compliance

Some stress-wise practices invite us to make space for quiet, stillness, and unencumbered breath and movement. But there is a difference between quiet stillness for *compliance* and quiet stillness for *contemplation*. Practices that integrate the body, mind, and heart are liberatory in that they are not required, but suggested. Allowing students to choose is fundamental to a stress-wise approach. This stands in sharp contrast to the traditional approach of mandated participation and predetermined outcomes. There are no right or wrong answers to the questions posed in stress-wise work; rather, we are asked to move beyond binary thinking and accept our different lived experiences with compassion. Students who are required to practice mindfulness may instead spend that time quietly ruminating and building tension, which is antithetical to the purpose.

Be aware of any perceived need for compliance among students. Remember, it is not only OK but also desirable for students to approach stress-wise practices in different ways. This means they are following their inner gauges to determine what is best for them in the moment, and that's what this work is all about. For some, moving away from compliance and uniformity will be the most challenging part of this work. We encourage you to trust the process and the creative ways that stress intelligence can emerge both individually and collectively.

# Safety Considerations

To ensure you create a classroom that is both inclusive and trauma-sensitive, we want to share some safety considerations that we have found to be helpful not just for students' physical health but also for their mental, emotional, and social wellness. We hope these illuminate and support your own ability to work within the stress-wise philosophy.

## First, Do No Harm

In the traditional philosophy of yoga, personal responsibilities are outlined before physical practice begins. One such responsibility—*ahimsa*, often translated from Sanskrit as "non-harming" or "nonviolence"—was key to Mahatma Gandhi's nonviolent liberation movement. Committing to not harming ourselves or others is a fundamental step in creating the safe environment necessary for student growth. In stress-wise classrooms, non-harming means allowing students to advocate for their needs, meeting them with equanimity, and encouraging them to develop self-compassion. Non-harming is a practice that begins within ourselves and expands outward into our relationships, systems, and society.

## Relative Safety

Race-equity trainer Michelle Cassandra Johnson describes the role of relative safety in cocreating effective learning environments (Johnson & Kelly, 2021). Although we cannot guarantee that any learning space is 100 percent safe, we can collaborate as learning communities to create safer spaces that allow us to take appropriate risks, move out of our comfort zones, and support one another to be brave (Arao & Clemens, 2013). Johnson reminds us that individuals face threats to their safety on the basis of race, class, gender, ability, political status, and other factors. Not everyone in a classroom experiences the same degree of safety, and our nervous systems respond differently to the same stimulus depending on our history, trauma, and mobility. Students who appear to be resisting participation may in fact be experiencing a lack of safety. Acknowledging these realities is critical to facilitating liberatory rather than oppressive practices. For white educators teaching students of color especially, developing cultural humility and committing to antiracism are crucial to creating a sense of safety in the classroom (Emdin, 2021; Hook et al., 2013; Magee, 2021; Tervalon & Murray-Garcia, 1998).

According to Stephen Porges's (2011) polyvagal theory, mindful practices like the ones in this book are most effective when students' social engagement systems (centered on the ventral vagal nerve) are activated. When we feel we can tolerate a situation—when we are in what Dan Siegel (1999) calls our "Window of Tolerance"—we are better able to engage in reflection and direct our attention willingly. In contrast, states of sympathetic arousal (the fight-or-flight response) or dorsal vagal activation (the freeze response) inhibit access to frontal lobe functions associated with mindfulness. Fortunately, mindful practices themselves can help us to modulate these different states and bring us into a Window of Tolerance. To ensure this happens safely, though, we must keep in mind the different states our students are in and proceed accordingly.

In his work on trauma-sensitive mindfulness, David Treleaven (Treleaven & Britton, 2018) teaches the importance of equipping students with ways to protect against unexpected encounters with inner turmoil resulting from trauma. These methods work like shields, allowing students to shift their attention from painful memories that may emerge during their mindfulness practice. We will introduce several shields in this book related to changing postures, redirecting attention to the senses, and accessing anchor points in the body. These skills allow students to practice mindfulness with confidence and agency. As facilitators, we can remind students that stress-wise praxis is intended to help us find more balance and health. Anytime we experience fear or heightened stress during mindfulness practice, we can choose to stop the practice and shift our awareness elsewhere. We call this a "wisdom shift." (The first LC in Chapter 1 guides students to identify their own personal wisdom shifts.)

## Accessibility

Though we have carefully and intentionally chosen practices that are broadly accessible, no single practice is always appropriate for every person. This is where your creativity and knowledge of your students are key. The goal is for each student to have an opportunity to engage in all the practices if they choose to do so. In mindful movement practices, the intent is generally for students to either connect breath and movement or notice the qualities of their movements to develop somatic awareness. If a student is not able to move in the exact way described in the practice, alternative strategies can be used. For example, if the instruction is to lift both arms overhead, students with limited mobility might lift only their hands and forearms or even just one finger.

## How to Provide Choice in Practice

Conscious choice-making is critical for stress-wise practitioners. Creating a culture of choice among your students will yield more participation and engagement while cultivating self-awareness and well-being. Contemplative practices like mindfulness and meditation simply cannot be forced, and trying to force them will only result in resistance and diminished trust. Here, then, are a few ways to encourage choice within the parameters of stress-wise LCs.

**Postural Choice:** All body-mind-heart practices include multiple options related to body posture, including sitting in a chair or on the floor, standing, or leaning against a wall. Sitting tall is a goal to aim for, but not a requirement. Some students will feel safer and more contained resting their heads on the desk or slouching with their arms and ankles crossed. We encourage you to let students move in ways that feel natural to them. What matters most is for students to develop a healthy, trusting relationship with their bodies.

**Alternative Activities:** It is advisable to have alternative activities in place for students who are not able or ready to engage in certain practices. Students who can identify and articulate unease with a practice are displaying self-awareness that we encourage you to reinforce by believing them and offering an alternative. Options can include writing, drawing, coloring, cleaning, resting, or anything else that might promote contemplation. Students who choose an alternative activity should respect their classmates' practices just as they would during any other assignment. Students who are initially apprehensive about a practice will often find their way into it over time as the language and experience become more familiar.

**Observation as Participation:** We want to provide multiple entry points into practice so that all students can make the choice to participate. One way to ensure this is to offer observation as a form of participation. There are two helpful guidelines to keep in mind when inviting this option. First, advise students to observe in a way that respects other classmates' privacy. Students can gaze in a neutral direction toward the floor or wall so that classmates do not feel they're being monitored during practice. If you are comfortable with it, you can even invite observers to keep their attention on you. Second, encourage observers to "hold space" for classmates. This means that an observing student is asked to protect the practice space by respecting the contemplative tone and vulnerability of the process. Student observers should maintain an open mind and compassionate heart as they hold space for their peers.

## Basic Supports

The following sections outline some ways to organize your students' experiences from a logistical perspective. Throughout the learning cycles, we will also offer suggestions for setting up your class to better facilitate the experience.

### Class Discussions

The Engage and Expand phases of learning cycles often include facilitated discussions. In some cases, a specific format is suggested. Otherwise, choose the format that works best for your class. (Circling is highly recommended at least once per LC to promote connections and equity.) Here are some options:

- **Casual group:** Students volunteer "popcorn" style or gesture to be called on.
- **Sequential circle:** Go around the circle and encourage each student to respond (with the option of passing).
- **Popcorn circle:** Students volunteer, then call on a volunteering classmate to respond next.

### Forming Small Groups

The Explore phase of each LC includes small-group work. Intentionally formulating groups and tracking their process is key to creating a useful experience for all students. Specific group formations are suggested for some activities, but for others you can try different formations to discover what works best for your class.

**Preliminary Considerations**

- Does your class have previously determined small groups that you would like to utilize for the purpose of stress-wise practice?
- If not, do you think your students will thrive in smaller groups of three, slightly larger groups of four or five, or a combination of groups that suit individual students' needs?

**Options**

- **Pre-selected:** Assign groups based on your knowledge and understanding of students.
- **Self-selected:** Students organize themselves. You may then choose to have students remain in the same groups for specific lengths of time or over a given number of LCs.
- **Random assembly:** Assign groups randomly.

**Roles**

Roles can be assigned in advance, or students can self-select them, and they can rotate through the group. The following roles are phased in over time:

- **Timekeeper:** makes sure the group is aware of time limits
- **Notetaker:** maintains the group's notes; delivers a copy to you when requested
- **Discussion facilitator:** makes sure everyone's voice and ideas are heard

## Materials

For many learning cycles, you will need some type of board for broadcasting information to the whole class (e.g., SMART Board, whiteboard, chalkboard, overhead projector). Students will need access to writing instruments and paper or digital methods of recording notes. Other basic supplies like index cards and chart paper can also support learning.

## Journals

Students will need a notebook throughout the stress-wise process. It is imperative that students know that these journals are not personal diaries and that you will be reviewing and responding to their work from time to time. Journals serve as an important communication tool between you and your students. We suggest reviewing journals monthly or at a frequency that supports your process in guiding students. Consider writing notes of encouragement and clarifying questions to deepen thinking as needed.

## Assessment

Assessment is baked into the phases of every learning cycle as follows.

### *Diagnostic Assessment*

- **Phase 1: Engage.** Students convey their learning and understanding through discussion and inquiry. In this diagnostic phase, you will be able to collect assessments through observation and listening.

### *Formative Assessment*

- **Phase 2: Explore.** Working in groups, students research, record, and report their findings. Monitoring, observing, and listening throughout activities will offer you insights into their individual and collective processes.
- **Phase 3: Embody.** Students have ongoing opportunities for self-assessment through body-mind-heart practices such as self-reflection. While you will be able to observe affect and tone during practice, check-ins afterward are essential to gauge students' experiences and make any needed adjustments. (Students track and log their process throughout phases 2 and 3.)
- **Phase 4: Expand.** Through presentation of science to further illustrate the mechanisms of action or evidence to support the topic from the LC as well as creative applications of stress-wise practices, students enter a stage of concept synthesis evidenced through further inquiry on the topic, asking more nuanced questions to further their own understanding and application. Formal and informal question-and-answer sessions provide opportunities for formative assessment.

*Summative Assessment*
- **Phase 5: Express.** Summative assessments take the form of journal entries, small-group presentations, creative writing, and artwork.

*Student Surveys*

Brief surveys featuring true-or-false, short-answer, and multiple-choice questions are offered at the end of each chapter. Consider using Google Forms or another convenient format for collecting responses.

## Evaluation

As a human development curriculum, the stress-wise framework focuses on enriching the quality of life for you and your students within and beyond the classroom. Unlike traditional academic subject areas, there are no rigid markers for grading in this model, though there are clear indicators of engagement and growth to look for in every phase of learning. We encourage you to support students' progress through brief narrative evaluations and by boldly acknowledging their courage, curiosity, and compassion. Student evaluations and communication with parents will deepen students' engagement and motivate them to integrate what they learn into their lives beyond school.

# Guiding Body-Mind-Heart Practices

We have explored the overarching philosophical concepts that inform how we can think about, approach, and facilitate stress-wise practice as well as the more practical ways of organizing the LCs with basic supports. The following sections outline some quintessential ways in which we can take care of ourselves, as the facilitators, and some ways to deliver the embodiment scripts without formal training in yoga, mindfulness, or contemplative practice.

## Center Yourself First

Your role in facilitating body-mind-heart practices is as important as your students' experience within it. As longtime facilitators, we cannot emphasize enough the importance of centering yourself before leading these experiences. Taking a few deep breaths, aligning your posture, or reading a short affirmation before beginning will go a long way toward ensuring that practices "land" for both you and your students.

## Pause

Pauses within scripts, guided experiences, and somatic practices allow the learner to get comfortable with being quiet in a mindful way, to reflect, and to touch base with the internal shifts that take place as awareness reorients from the external to the internal dimension. Pauses also give the facilitator time to breathe, get grounded, and sense any collective shifts in energy, demeanor, or vitality within the classroom.

## Consider Voice/Prosody

In addition to *what* we say, *how* we say it communicates and instructs. During embodiment practices, your voice serves as a guide and narrator of internal experience rather than as a lecturer or entertainer. Pitch and volume are more regulated, intonation is dialed down, and speech is delivered deliberately and with more rhythm, allowing the listener to follow along in a self-reflective way.

## Pace Yourself

Pacing is pivotal. Speaking too quickly or unclearly may strain listeners or put pressure on them to respond prematurely. Deliberate pacing gives listeners the space and time they need to learn how to listen to their inherent voices of wisdom. Tension doesn't always require immediate relief. These practices are designed to take us beyond our comfort zones and into self-discovery. Pace experiences in a way that allows students to arrive naturally at their own discoveries.

## Slowly In, Slowly Out

Like a shaken snow globe, these practices require time for their internal systems to settle. A slow, deliberate transition out of internal focus helps students reorient themselves with their outer surroundings and peers and helps them remain grounded.

# Make It Your Own

The more connected you feel to the content, the more able you will be to draw your students into the process of developing stress intelligence. Please feel free and empowered to do the following:

- Rephrase questions to fit your and your students' sensibilities.
- Adjust delivery methods to meet your classroom needs.
- Adapt stories and examples for cultural relevance.
- Use alternative metaphors that resonate more with your students.

### Repetition Works

Repeat the practices that work well for your classroom. We have provided a variety of tools and techniques for your stress-wise toolbox that you can use across your diverse group of learners. If there are practices in the following chapters that speak loudly and clearly to your group, use them often. Repetition works to reinforce techniques and allows for greater depth of learning. What works on repeat one school year might not the next year, and that is OK, too.

## Educator Reflection

We invite you to pause for a moment and remember a time in your life when you felt inspired, strong, and energized. Take your time reflecting before deciding on a particular memory. Welcome this memory closer. For a few moments, investigate these questions:

- How do you remember feeling in your body at that time of your life?
- How do you feel in your body right now, while recalling this memory?
- Would you describe the experience you remembered as one of vitality? If not, what words would you use to describe it?
- Thinking back, was your life completely free of stress during this time?

Chances are you answered no to that last question. The truth is, stress and vitality coexist. A deeper understanding of both can help educators and students find inspiration, strength, and restored energy in the classroom. Knowing and reminding ourselves of this basic fact is at the heart of this exploration.

# 2

# Know: Exploring Stress and Vitality in the Classroom Through the Scope of Awareness

*The moment one gives close attention to anything, even a blade of grass, it becomes a mysterious, awesome, indescribably magnificent world in itself.*

—Henry Miller

> **Guiding Question**
> How can educators provide opportunities for students to know when they are experiencing stress and to nurture vitality?

In a stress-wise classroom, your goal is to cultivate and sustain an environment where creativity, compassion, and well-being can thrive for both you and your students. The first step of developing stress intelligence is to know when you are experiencing stress and when you are experiencing vitality—and to understand *how* you know these things. How do you know when your students are stressed? What signals do your students give you that indicate they feel stressed? The learning cycles in this chapter provide multiple opportunities for you and your students to bring awareness to the physical, mental, emotional, and social signs of stress and vitality.

## What Is Stress?

The National Institute of Mental Health (2021) defines stress as "how the brain and body respond to any demand." Stress is a physiological response to stimuli—environmental, psychosocial, physical, economic, emotional, and beyond. Stress is a necessary part of life, essential for growth and change; and like life, it is also cyclical. When we experience stress in a healthy way, we move through its cycles without getting stuck in any phase of it, discharge our stressful energy, and return our system to homeostasis, or relatively steady equilibrium (Peters et al., 2017). Unfortunately, too many of us experience stress in an unhealthy way that leaves the stress cycle unresolved, raises our baseline levels of stress, and can eventually lead to chronic stress. A state of continual stress drains us physically, overstimulates us mentally, and prevents us from accessing such feelings as joy, awareness, compassion, and equanimity, all of which lead to greater vitality. Some signs of chronic stress include the following:

- Low energy, fatigue, and troubled sleep
- Digestive discomforts (e.g., constipation, loose stools, gas, bloating, heartburn) and appetite changes
- Aches and pains
- Frequent colds or coughs
- Trouble regulating body temperature
- Restlessness, anxiety, or fearful thinking
- Unfocused or cloudy thinking, inability to retain information
- Feeling overwhelmed, unmotivated, depressed, or withdrawn

Thankfully, there are ways to ensure that we experience stress in as healthy a way as possible. Body-mind-heart practices help us to complete cycles of stress, allowing for integration of the stressor, increased awareness, and greater resilience in the face of future stress.

# What Is Vitality?

The word *vitality* is derived from the Latin *vitalis,* meaning "of or belonging to life." Like stress, vitality is intrinsic to all living beings, affecting how all of us grow and develop. Robert Thayer (1987) describes vitality as "the relaxed possession of liveliness and vigor." In the classroom, vitality feels like vigor, inspiration, and aliveness. Part of stress intelligence is understanding that both stress and vitality are necessary to learning.

Signs and symptoms of vitality include the following:

- Feeling refreshed upon waking
- Sleeping through the night
- Feeling energized after eating
- Experiencing curiosity, joy, and compassion for others
- Feeling connected to loved ones
- Wanting to move your body
- Feeling ready to take on a challenge

How do you detect vitality in your students? What are the signals?

# The Scope of Awareness

Helping learners develop stress intelligence starts with awareness. Guiding students to become more aware is like showing them the light switch in a darkened room: Once they know where it is, they can turn it on at will.

## The Hidden Power of Awareness

Like breathing, awareness tends to function at a subconscious level and only emerge when something goes wrong—that is, when we realize we have been *unaware*. How many times do we remind students to "be more aware" *after* the fall, collision, or hurtful speech? As teachers, our aim should be to nurture the kind of self-knowledge in students that literally brings learning to life.

In her book *Peace from Anxiety* (2021), our inspirational colleague Hala Khouri refers to the body as a personal navigation system. She describes how we make meaning in life by taking in stimuli from the outer world and responding to internal stimuli. "Our first step in working with anxiety is understanding our body," she explains, "how it's feeling, where the sensations come from, and how we can navigate these feelings" (p. 1). We gain this understanding by cultivating somatic awareness, or the mindful noticing of the feeling of our body (Schwartz, 2017). Awareness grants us access to the information our body consistently communicates to us. Once we become aware of these messages, we can more easily navigate life and better appreciate the magnificent systems within us. The body serves as a grounding rod for the elusive subject of awareness.

## Stress IQ Is Mindful

We are often invited to consult with school communities that are all too aware of the stress they are facing and frustrated when stress-reduction efforts don't work or even backfire. In many cases, we find that the remedy involves intentionally shifting the quality of awareness that leaders and teachers bring to the process of reducing stress. Educators and students are fully aware of the systemic stresses involved in education. When we only focus on the larger issue of systemic stress, however, our awareness can become hijacked by challenges beyond our immediate control, leaving us feeling too drained to deal with the challenges right in front of us. Awareness exists on a spectrum between hypervigilant and diffuse, and different levels are useful in different situations. In classrooms, teachers should seek to cultivate *mindful* awareness focused on the present moment.

Mindful awareness does not mean ignoring systemic issues but, rather, claiming our agency. Sometimes the most powerful lever of change available to us consists of our own inner awareness of ourselves. When we realize our power to shift and harness the quality of our awareness, we transform ourselves and, by extension, our learning environments. We want to harness the power of mindful awareness to disarm the structures that impose debilitating stress on our communities and transform the social conditions that consistently threaten the well-being of our students.

A stress-wise approach to the classroom looks like Marisol, who greets her students with kindness and without judgment every single day. It also looks like Dante, who has developed a keen sense of his students' emotional states and is willing to walk them outside for some fresh air and sunshine when they need a fresh start. It looks like Kimberly, a veteran educator who realized her reactivity to stress was unsustainable and reframed her approach to include weekly deep-rest practice with her students.

In *your* classroom, the stress-wise approach will look like a unique expression of you and your students. The key is to develop an awareness that is curious, caring, and nonjudgmental. Of course, this takes practice—just as it took practice for Marisol, Dante, and Kimberly. They made mistakes. They reflected. And they began again, over and over. Every phase in every learning cycle is an opportunity to practice applying mindful awareness in your teaching.

When we are mindfully aware, we consciously pay attention to what is taking place within and around us. In this way, awareness can function as a regulator. Slowing us down enough to face the present with a sense of curiosity creates space for us to attend to our needs more effectively. Mindful awareness helps us to become more compassionate toward ourselves by seeing our stress as part of our shared humanity. To become aware of awareness and to examine it is to enter a mystery that has practical implications for learning communities.

When students are mindfully aware, they know the following:

- When they need a "bio break" to care for their bodies' needs
- When they need a brain break to refresh their thought process
- What their strongest learning styles are
- What modes of expression feel the most alive and inspiring to them
- When they've lost focus and need to cultivate concentration

Going forward, we encourage you to utilize your own scope of awareness to gauge levels of stress and vitality in your classroom. When you notice stress levels rising during testing season, before a big presentation, or because a "real world" circumstance is burdening your students, say so, and invite students to do the same. If the first step of becoming stress wise is awareness, then the first step of taming stress is naming it. Sometimes the simple act of acknowledging that stress is present can invoke coregulation, so call out the elephant in the room and watch the collective atmosphere change.

Likewise, when you notice a sense of vitality in your students or even yourself, say so! Celebrate and appreciate the sparks of well-being as they arise. Remember, stress intelligence is about enhancing overall well-being in yourself and your students. Although it can be easy to slip into an acute awareness of stress and forget to notice the good times, bringing awareness to any sense of vitality, no matter how small, will help it grow. Think about how you will celebrate the next time your students show up with positive energy and vitality. Simply naming the positivity aloud is an easy way to reinforce well-being.

Though vitality and gratitude are essential to well-being, we are in no way guiding you over the "good vibes only" edge. All humans have a psychological bias to notice what is problematic or potentially problematic and to prevent it or react to it quickly. Actively acknowledging what is working well and what feels great can help you to balance this bias and cultivate a wider scope of awareness in which we can show up as whole humans connected to our shared humanity in the classroom setting (Hanson, 2019).

# Learning Cycle 1: Stress-Wise Basics

**Objectives**
- Introduce the concept of stress intelligence and the stress-wise framework.
- Affirm students' aspirations, admirations, and aptitudes.
- Identify inner resources to support students during body-mind-heart practice.

**Outcomes**
- Students will recognize the capacity to shift awareness at will.
- Students will connect to inherent traits of wisdom.

**Keywords:** *wisdom, aspiration, modulate, stress, intelligence, praxis*

> **From Abby's Classroom**
>
> I use models and illustrations of body systems as visual aids in my classroom, which can frighten and disgust some students. One fall day, a student named Janelle walked into our classroom and noticed that Mr. Bones, our class skeleton, had been brought out of the closet for the first time that year. "Ah! No! Scary!" she shrieked. "Why is that thing in here?"
>
> Amused, I replied, "You have a 'thing' like that in your own body that is with you all the time. Has your own skeleton ever scared you?"
>
> Janelle was taken aback. "You know, Miss, I never thought about it that way," she said. "Skeletons come out at Halloween, and I always think of them as dead. But I guess my skeleton is alive?" This new awareness led to a vitalizing lesson exploring the fact that our skeletons are not only alive but also essential to our own lives.

# Phase 1.1: Engage
## Natural Wisdom: Find Out What Students Already Know

**Timeframe:** 10–20 minutes

**Class Discussion**

Start by introducing the stress-wise framework to your students. How you do this is ultimately up to you and will likely change over time. Here are a few ideas to support you:

1. Let students know that you have been reading this book and want to share some of the activities and practices you are learning about.
2. Acknowledge that life is stressful, so you are making time for the class to tend to their personal and collective well-being.
3. Let students know that stress management is supported by science and that you will be exploring how to be stress wise together.

Next, use one or all three of the following open-ended inquiries to prompt discussion:

- What is wisdom?
- Where does wisdom come from?
- Who do you know among your family, community, or friends who is wise?

Encourage students to answer with whatever thoughts come to their minds. Let them know you are not looking for a "right" answer but, rather, are interested in their thoughts on the topic. While guiding the discussion, acknowledge and point out connections between students' responses.

Now switch gears with one of the following prompts:

- Who has experienced stress in the past few months, weeks, or days? Who is experiencing it right now?
- What would you like to know more about how to deal with stress in your life?
- What *is* stress, anyway?

Let students know the class will be exploring these questions and more as you work together to become stress wise.

## Phase 1.2: Explore. Becoming Aware of Our Assets

**Timeframe:** 20 minutes

Students commonly respond to the topic of stress much as Janelle did to the skeleton in Abby's classroom: by recoiling from it. To temper this response, it's best to enter the exploration of stress slowly and deliberately, beginning with building awareness of what is good in students' lives—what Trabian Shorters calls "asset framing" (Tippett, 2022). When Janelle focused awareness on her own skeleton, she ceased to be frightened of the classroom model. In the same way, equipping students with a keener awareness of their strengths and assets helps them to develop their stress IQ.

**Small-Group Activity**

Follow these steps with students:

1. Let students know they will be meeting in small groups to research topics.
2. Once groups are formed, task students with defining the following three terms: *aspirations, attributes,* and *aptitudes.*
3. Students list people who possess attributes and aptitudes they aspire to have.
4. For each person listed, students answer the question "What is it about this person that you aspire to?"

5. Students answer the question "If your group were on a ship together, what would the name of the ship be?" This answer becomes the name of the group.
6. Each group shares its group name and two or three people from its list with the whole class.

Although simple on the surface, this activity gives your students an opportunity to consider and share their assets—in this case, the people in their lives who possess attributes and aptitudes they aspire to embody. This kind of empowerment and strength-building is the foundation on which stress IQ is built. Once you know what students aspire to, you can continue to draw on that information to motivate growth. For example, when Abby conducted this activity in her classroom, Janelle shared that she aspired to be a clothing designer. In turn, Abby shared that the designer Stella McCartney uses meditation to navigate stress and anxiety.

## Phase 1.3: Embody
### Choosing a Shift: A Tool for Shifting from Stress to Safety

**Timeframe:** 10 minutes

Being introspective and paying conscious attention to emotional experiences requires a level of vulnerability that may cause some students to feel exposed or disoriented. To support student safety and agency, we encourage implementing "wisdom shifts" during stress-wise practice. A wisdom shift refers to the process of shifting attention toward a chosen thought, image, or sensory experience when one is feeling overwhelmed.

In this phase of the learning cycle, you will guide students to identify a personal wisdom shift. Let them know that you will be guiding practices designed to help them connect with their bodies, minds, and hearts, and that they can choose to either participate or observe. The only rule is that they don't interrupt or distract classmates during practice time.

Guide the practice using your own words or the following script:

Find a comfortable position for your body. Choose to either close your eyes or fix a soft gaze in one direction below the horizon. Pause for a few breaths.

Now, reflect on your own natural wisdom. What are you naturally interested in that makes you unique? [Pause.] What are your aptitudes? [Pause.] What are your gifts? [Pause.]

During practice times like this, you are the captain of your own boat. You can shift direction or take a break whenever you need to. If a practice feels overwhelming, you can shift your attention to a person, place, or thing that helps you to feel stable. This is called a *wisdom shift*, and it could be any of the following:

- One of your gifts or interests
- A person, place, or animal you love
- An image that helps you feel present (can be anything!)
- A part of nature that helps you feel steady, such as a tree, a mountain, or the sky

What can you bring your attention to when you need to find more stability or take a break from a practice? [Pause.] Slowly start to bring your awareness back to the space around you. Take a few moments to acclimate back into the space we all share.

**Post-Practice Check-In**

Once the practice is completed, ask students if they were able to identify a wisdom shift. If the concept isn't clear to them yet, ask for a student volunteer to explain what they heard. You can also further clarify as follows: "If you find yourself uneasy during a practice, remember your wisdom shift. With your shift, you can slow down, speed up, or take a break from the practice."

Just about anything that helps a student feel grounded or balanced can be a wisdom shift. For Janelle, looking at her shoes (always ultra-clean and polished) and wiggling her toes was a way to bring herself back to the present moment when she felt her attention wandering into worry.

## Phase 1.4: Expand. Bird's-Eye View of Stress-Wise Praxis

**Timeframe:** 20 minutes

**Materials:** Figure 1.2

Now that students have started to make connections to their innate wisdom and aspirations, it's time to provide more definitions and an outlook of their stress-wise journey. Please use the following definitions, descriptions, and figure to offer your students an orientation to stress intelligence, stress-wise praxis, and the six-mode stress-wise framework. You may read the text aloud as written, or paraphrase it in your own words.

### Defining Stress Intelligence

Stress intelligence or stress IQ involves accepting stress as a natural and necessary part of life that we can learn to relate with in ways that support our personal and collective well-being.

### Stress-Wise Praxis

Stress-wise praxis is about tapping into our inner wisdom and developing our stress intelligence. *Praxis* means working together to change what is not working for us and create a healthier situation for everyone. This includes the following:

- Small- and whole-group activities, research, and discussions
- Body-mind-heart practices related to mindfulness, visualization, breathing, movement, and resting
- Learning about the science and physiology of stress, vitality, and well-being
- Expressing your learning through journaling, art, and presentations

### Six-Mode Stress-Wise Framework

Now share the six modes of the stress-wise framework with students. Show them Figure 1.2 (see p. 7) and use the following explanations to describe each mode.

1. **Know:** We are aware when stress and vitality are present.
2. **Differentiate:** We know the difference between helpful and harmful stress.
3. **Identify:** We know the sources of stress and vitality in our lives.
4. **Discern:** We make wise choices for our well-being.
5. **Resource:** We care for ourselves and each other.
6. **Relate:** We hear, see, and support each other.

Let students know that the word *modulate* comes from the Latin word *modulus,* meaning to adapt, change, regulate, or alleviate. In music, modulation means a change of one tone or key to another. What do you think *modulate* means in reference to stress?

Invite questions. Let students know that you may not be answering every question at this very moment, but that their questions will lead the way for further exploration.

### Phase 1.5: Express. Wisdom Share

**Timeframe:** 20 minutes

Ask students to recall the wisdom shift they chose in Phase 1.3. If they need a reminder or more time, revisit that phase.

In their journals, students list as many of their gifts, skills, talents, interests, and aptitudes as they can think of in three to four minutes. Encourage them to include everything that comes to mind, even abstractions like colors, sounds, smells, places, and parts of nature that help them to feel strong.

Next, students choose one item from the list they feel most connected to right now and write it down on the other side of their journal page. Give them five minutes or more to create and decorate their "wisdom shift" words.

When students are finished, invite them to share using the phrase "I am [word on their sheet] wise."

# Learning Cycle 2: Cultivating Awareness

**Objectives**
- Engage students in contemplation and dialogue on the meaning of awareness.
- Explore how the body communicates basic needs.
- Develop mindful awareness through sensory practices.

**Outcomes**
- Students will activate awareness as a tool for knowing.
- Students will know the functions of interoceptive, exteroceptive, and somatic awareness.

**Keywords:** *awareness, interoception, exteroception, somatic awareness*

> **From Niki's Classroom**
>
> In a course Niki designed called "Relaxation Residency," a group of high school seniors were preparing to graduate from a rigorous medical magnet school program. The goal of the course was for students to develop relaxation skills they could use during this stressful time in their lives. On day one, Niki shared with her students that stress is something we all have in common and that we need to put in the effort to relate to it in a healthy way (Saccareccia, 2017). Before class was to begin with guided breathing practice, a friendly and extroverted student named Angel introduced himself to Niki and mentioned how excited he was to learn how to meditate. He had heard how helpful it could be for dealing with anxiety. He shared that he would be the first in his family to attend college, and that although he found this exciting, he found the pressure to succeed challenging.
>
> Niki led Angel and his 30 classmates through a simple guided meditation on noticing the feeling of breathing, progressively moving from awareness of breathing to awareness of different parts of their bodies in a systematic practice called "body scanning." It didn't take very long for this group to find a quietude necessary for deep focus. After about 15 minutes, Niki prompted her students to bring their awareness back into the shared space, noticing sounds from their classmates and any ambient noise in the room as they gradually reopened their eyes.
>
> When the session had ended and students had moved on to their next class activity, Angel pulled Niki aside to share his first experience of mindful awareness: "When I opened my eyes, it's like the world was in HD. Like the default world before was so dull and out of focus. Now, everything is so much clearer!"

## Phase 2.1: Engage. Locating Awareness

**Timeframe:** 10–20 minutes

**Class Discussion** (5–15 minutes)

Lead your class through an open-ended discussion to bring their thoughts and ideas on awareness to the surface. Use one or more of the following prompts to begin the discussion:

- What is awareness?
- Where in the world is awareness?
- Where does awareness come from?

The goal of this discussion is to give you a baseline of your students' understanding and to evoke interest in the topic of awareness. Acknowledge and affirm your students' ideas without feeling the need to assess them. Here is some more information to support your use of the above prompts:

- **What is awareness?** Merriam-Webster defines *awareness* as "the quality or state of being aware: knowledge and understanding that something is happening and exists." To be aware is to know, or the state of knowing. Our awareness is a powerful resource in our learning and our lives.
- **Where in the world is awareness?** This is an intentionally enigmatic question meant to provide students an opportunity to wonder. You might ask them to look for their awareness. Can they find it? Can they describe it?
- **Where does awareness come from?** Awareness is a basic human capacity. We do not need to create it or go out and get it. An unlimited supply of awareness is always available to us.

To conclude the discussion, invite students to complete the sentence stem "Awareness is _____." Encourage them to say whatever comes to mind. Call for a volunteer to record responses on the board or on a piece of paper. Students may offer responses like these:

Awareness is . . .

- Everywhere and nowhere.
- What the mind does.
- Invisible.
- Knowing what's up.
- A mystery.

**Sensory Awareness Practice** (3–4 minutes)

Our senses are useful tools for directing awareness. Let students know you will be guiding them through a series of prompts that utilize their sense of sight. You may use or adapt the following script:

Everyone, please allow your eyes to wander around the room and locate something orange. Pause to notice the shape of the object. [Pause.]

Let your eyes roam again. Locate a blue object. Pause to notice any texture in the blue object. [Pause for a little longer than before.]

Now gaze slowly around the room to find a green object. [Pause.] What do you notice about the green object? Let your gaze and your awareness remain on the green object for the next 20–30 seconds. When you notice your eyes start to wander, simply guide your awareness back to the green object. [Pause for 20–30 seconds.]

Finally, let your sight wander around the room until you become aware of a color that is pleasing to you. Pause and gaze at the object. How do you know you like this color? Is there a feeling in your body or a thought that arises letting you know it is a pleasing color? Does the color remind you of anything? [Pause for 30 or more seconds.]

OK, now let go of focusing your awareness on individual objects and take in the whole room again, including the people around you.

**Process and Gauge** (2–3 minutes)

Invite students to share what they noticed in the sensory awareness practice. Ask them if they found this practice helpful for tuning their awareness into the present moment. Note students' ability to engage in practice and express their experience:

- Who seems to be open and receptive?
- Who seems to be resistant or apprehensive?
- Does anyone appear to be confused about the practice?

# Phase 2.2: Explore
## Thirst Games: How Do We Know We Are Thirsty?

**Timeframe:** 20 minutes

**Small-Group Activity**

Before beginning this activity, assign or invite a volunteer in each group to serve as timekeeper.

1. Ask students to answer the question "How do we know when we are thirsty?"
2. Students discuss and list the physical signs of thirst on paper. This is an exploration of the group members' own lived experiences.
3. Next, students research the mechanics of thirst online. They can come up with their own thirst-related questions to begin their research or use the question you provided. Each group locates and notes at least one interesting fact about thirst to share with the group.
4. A representative from each group reports out their findings to the class.

End this activity by pointing out how much is going on within our bodies and the world around us that we are often unaware of.

The next activity will help students to become more aware of what is happening within their own bodies. Recall that a skeleton was once scary to Janelle but became normal to her once she became aware that she was living with one of her own.

## Phase 2.3: Embody
### Food on the Mind: Inner Awareness Exercise

**Timeframe:** 10 minutes

**Body-Mind-Heart Practice** (5 minutes)

Invite students to sit or lie down comfortably. Guide them through this experience as follows:

> If it feels comfortable for you, close your eyes or maintain a soft focus. Take a few deep breaths, in through the nose and out through the mouth. [Pause.]
>
> Imagine that your favorite food is right here in front of you. Picture the colors and shape of your favorite food. Can you imagine

the smell of the food? Does it make your mouth water? Are there any positive memories associated with it?

Where in your body can you feel the excitement and anticipation of seeing your favorite food? How would you feel if a friend or loved one brought you this food? Would you smile? If so, try smiling now.

As you come back from thinking about this food, consider how it impacted your mood. How did you feel while thinking about your favorite food? Did you feel happy? Hungry? How else did you feel?

**Triad Shares** (5 minutes)

Allow students time to share about the practice in triads. Provide the following prompts on the board:

- What did you notice during the practice?
- How do you know when you are happy?
- How do your thoughts impact how you feel?

## Phase 2.4: Expand. Ways of Knowing, Inside and Out

**Timeframe:** 20 minutes

There are many ways of knowing, or ways to access our awareness. Our senses provide direct access to knowing and are even called "wisdom channels" in the yogic tradition. Ask students to name the five senses we typically refer to.

Next, it's time to examine two additional kinds of awareness that have been used so far in this learning cycle: *interoception* and *exteroception*. Write the following definitions on the board and invite a volunteer to read each one aloud:

- **Interoception** refers to perception of sensations from inside the body, including physical sensations such as thirst, hunger, heartbeat, breathing, and emotions.
- **Exteroception** refers to any sensation that results from stimuli located outside the body and is detected by exteroceptors, including vision, hearing, touch or pressure, heat, cold, pain, smell, and taste.

Ask students, "Can you feel your breath moving inside of your body? Where do you feel it?" Janelle was able to feel her breath expanding in her rib cage, creating a gentle "pop" in her back. This level of interoception helps us to notice the internal signs of stress.

Say to students, "Notice the feeling of the air on your skin. Is it cool, cold, warm, or hot? As you move through your day, be aware of how the sensations in your body change in different situations. Noticing the messages your body sends through exteroception is called somatic awareness."

The following activity can be based on visualization or use real drinks. If the latter, each student will need one warm beverage (e.g., hot water) and one cold beverage (e.g., iced water). You can use the following script:

> Sit comfortably. Notice how your body feels internally. Is it warm or cool? Notice how your body feels externally. Is it warm or cool?
>
> As you hold a cold drink in your hands, what do you notice change in your body? How far up your arms can you feel the sensation of cold? Does it change the temperature of your body? How does it affect your mood?
>
> As you hold a warm drink in your hands, what do you notice change in your body? How far up your arms can you feel the sensation of warmth? Does it change the temperature of your body? How does it affect your mood?
>
> Based on this activity, how do you think interoception and exteroception affect each other? What did you learn about your body's awareness of temperature?

## Phase 2.5: Express. "Right Now I Know" Wisdom Share

**Timeframe:** 5–10 minutes

**Journaling Prompts**

Ask students to follow these steps:

1. List or draw a picture of three to five sensations you can detect *inside* your body.

2. List or draw a picture of three to five sensations you perceive from *outside* your body, including at least one sight, one sound, and one smell.
3. Complete the sentence stem: "Right now, I know _____." Here are some examples:
    - I'm hungry.
    - It's almost time to go home.
    - Something smells good.
    - I'm tired.
    - I'm in love.

Next, say, "Our awareness is our own. No one can own our awareness. Once we know that our awareness is within our power, we are better able to make choices about who and what we focus on and where our attention goes. When we learn to direct our awareness, we learn to direct our lives."

# Learning Cycle 3
# Gaining Perspective on Stress

**Objectives**
- Define *stress, distress, vitality,* and *well-being.*
- Investigate and experience the body-mind-heart connection.
- Use the stress–vitality spectrum as a tool for students to deepen awareness of personal and collective states of being.

**Outcomes**
- Students will increase their ability to use awareness as a tool for knowing when they are experiencing stress.
- Students will recognize the physical, mental, social, and emotional signs of stress and vitality.
- Students will enhance their capacity to assess and name energy levels.

**Keywords:** *stress, distress, vitality, well-being, energy, centered*

## Phase 3.1: Engage. Stress and Vitality Coexist

**Timeframe:** 20 minutes

**Materials:** posterboard or chart paper, pens or pencils

**Brainstorm** (7–10 minutes)

Write the words *stress, distress, vitality,* and *well-being* on four separate posters and place them around the room. Then ask students to pair up and move from poster to poster, writing their thoughts on or definitions for each word directly on the poster. Once the posters are populated with students' thoughts and ideas, call on volunteers to read the responses aloud.

It's always exciting to learn what students think about these topics. Look for students to notice the difference between stress and distress. Make note of what students share about vitality and well-being so that you can build these ideas into the stress-wise process. For example, Janelle shared that, for her, well-being includes taking walks with her sister. When Abby would notice Janelle's energy waning, she'd suggest a walk to connect with her sister as a way to recharge.

## Phase 3.2: Explore. How Stress and Vitality Show Up

**Timeframe:** 20 minutes

**Small-Group Activity**

Students assemble into four groups, each of which is assigned one of the following categories:

1. Physical signs of stress and vitality
2. Emotional signs of stress and vitality
3. Mental signs of stress and vitality
4. Social signs of stress and vitality

Provide these prompts and ask students to use their assigned categories to respond to them:

- How do we know when we are stressed? What are the signals of stress?
- How do we know when we are thriving? What are the signals of vitality?

When students are done, each group presents its findings to the rest of the class. (Note: If students have a hard time naming signs of vitality, share a few of the ones from the "What Is Vitality?" section of this chapter.)

## Phase 3.3: Embody. Knowing What Works for Us

**Timeframe:** 7–10 minutes

**Materials:** amplified music with volume control

**Peace Pause Practice** (5 minutes)

Talking about stress can be stressful, but by becoming more aware, we gain control over how we experience stress. In this phase, you and your students will explore a simple practice to feel the difference between stress and vitality, learn how to find the "sweet spot" of tolerable stress, and understand how to pause when necessary and find peace.

Before you begin, remind students of the choice they have to employ a wisdom shift anytime a practice feels overwhelming.

Tell students that you are going to turn on a song for everyone to listen to. Encourage them to listen mindfully and give you a peace sign or thumbs up when the volume is at the perfect level for them. Start by playing the song very quietly, then suddenly turn it up loudly, waiting for your students' response. Continue to fluctuate between soft, loud, and medium volume until most students give you the gesture indicating the sweet spot. When this happens, acknowledge it and give some time for everyone to enjoy the music at the chosen volume. Then, pause the song and lead the following awareness-building practice:

Think about the symbol on a pause button: two parallel lines with a space between them. If possible, place your feet in the shape of the pause symbol on the floor. Scoot forward in your chair or stand up and place your feet on the floor. [Pause.]

Let your eyes soften and gaze in one direction toward the ground.

For a few moments, bring your awareness to the soles of your feet. Pause to feel your feet on the ground. Notice how your feet feel. Feel the earth beneath your feet. [Pause.]

Now shift your awareness to the palms of your hands. Notice the feeling of your hands. Can you relax your hands a little bit? [Pause.]

Finally, can you remember a peaceful moment in your life when you felt free or at ease? Or maybe you can think about a peaceful sound or song. Let your mind and body pause to remember what peace feels like for a moment. [Pause.]

Breathe a sense of peace into your body. Relax your face a little bit. Let a peaceful feeling linger in your awareness for a few more moments. [Pause for 10–30 seconds or more.]

Slowly bring your awareness back to your hands, then to your feet, and then to the room and people around you. Remember: Pausing to find peace is a practice. It may feel strange or awkward at first, but over time, you might find that taking a peaceful pause can help to alleviate stress.

**Process and Gauge (3 minutes or more)**

Invite students to share what came to mind when remembering a peaceful moment, sound, or song. Ask them to flash a peace sign or a thumbs up if that practice felt OK, a thumbs down if the practice did not feel OK, and a sideways thumb for neutral.

Now put the music back on and let students move and dance!

## Phase 3.4: Expand. Knowing Our Limits

**Timeframe:** 10 minutes

**Materials (optional):** yarn or string, posterboard or chart paper

Write the words *hyper, exhausted,* and *centered* on posters (one word per poster). Post the ones that say *hyper* and *exhausted* on opposite walls. At the midway point between them, post the one that says *centered*.

Either have students visualize an imaginary beam connecting the three words on a spectrum or run a length of yarn or string along the entire length of the room, connecting the words. Use these prompts to guide discussion:

- What does *hyper* feel like?
- What does *exhausted* feel like?
- What does it mean to feel *centered?*
- How is your energy level right now?

Invite students to concentrate mindfully by following this script:

> Find a comfortable posture to be in for a few moments where your body feels calm and your mind can focus. Imagine a wide beam of light that starts out as a deep blue color and gradually becomes a bright red color. See the area where the blue color turns a little purple and then eventually becomes more red. Label the blue zone *exhaustion,* the purple zone *centered,* and the red zone *hyper.*
>
> Now bring awareness to your body. Sense what your body is sitting on and resting against. Can you sense your clothes touching your body? Take a moment to notice. Can you notice your body breathing? Feel yourself breathing. Does your body generally feel exhausted, centered, or hyper right now? Make a mental note about what you observe.
>
> Now bring awareness to your mind. Where does your mind belong? Is it part of your body, or does it feel like it's somewhere else? Does it have many thoughts right now, or just a few? Does it feel exhausted, centered, or hyper right now?
>
> OK, now what about your heart, the part of you that is loving, considerate, ethical, and kind—how does your heart feel at this moment? Does it feel exhausted, centered, or hyper right now?
>
> Take a few moments to rest. It may feel good to take two or three deep breaths and sigh away the exhales. Then, open your eyes or lift your gaze, noticing the room and your classmates. Now stand or sit near the poster that best reflects how your body, mind, and heart are feeling right now.

**Name the Center Zone**

In small groups, students brainstorm different ideas of what being centered feels like. Guide them as follows:

> What words or feelings come to mind when you think of the word *centered?* Be creative. Look to nature and art for clues. Is there a song, sound, or color that expresses the feeling of being centered or balanced? What name would your group give to the central zone? Write your group's words on a sheet of paper.

Groups then share their words with the whole class and place them in the center zone of the spectrum. Here are some possible sample responses:

- The sun
- Chill zone
- The stamen
- What's good

## Phase 3.5: Express. Stress IQ Check-In

**Timeframe:** 10 minutes

Issue the following survey in Google Forms or another convenient format for collecting responses. Be sure to let students know this is not a test—the intention of the survey is to check for understanding before moving forward into the next mode of the stress-wise framework. The survey allows students to share with you what they have learned and what has been useful to them. If students point to a particular exercise as having been useful, consider repeating that exercise more often as a "go-to" stress-wise practice.

The survey questions are as follows:

1. Does stress intelligence mean you can make all stress go away if you try hard enough? ___Yes ___ No
2. Are you open to learning more about how to be stress wise? ___Yes ___ No

3. Complete this sentence:
   "I know I am experiencing stress when _____."
4. Which of the following are signs of vitality? Check all that apply:
   ___ Waking up feeling refreshed
   ___ Feeling energized after eating
   ___ Worrying about things I cannot control
   ___ Experiencing curiosity, joy, and compassion for others
   ___ Engaging in negative self-talk
5. What are three ways you can recharge when you feel drained?
   a. _____
   b. _____
   c. _____

These questions are intentionally pointed to give you an opportunity to clarify misconceptions. For example, if students answer yes to the first question, be sure to clarify that there is no way to make all stress go away. Let students know that the goal of developing stress intelligence is to learn to live with the inevitable stressors of life in healthy ways that promote well-being.

The second question gives you a sense of students' personal experience with the process: Are they feeling open to learning more or not? Knowing this will help inform your approach going forward. Celebrate students who are open to the stress-wise process while acknowledging that some students may be struggling to engage. Simply giving students this chance to be honest with you about their experience can help to alleviate pressure. When we are invited to teach a modality like mindfulness with a new group of adolescents, we often start by asking, "What would you rather be doing?" Not only do we learn about students' interests right away, but we also put them at ease by acknowledging those who feel uneasy about a strange new experience. From there, we can encourage openness while respecting and meeting students where they actually are.

The third and fourth questions let you know whether students are developing an awareness of the signs of both stress and vitality. If you have students who are not able to answer these questions, consider inviting students who *are* able to read their answers aloud. Sometimes hearing a classmate's responses can elicit understanding.

Finally, the fifth question can become a working list of practices and activities to implement when you notice a drop in your students' energy. When students feel seen and heard in this way, deeper trust emerges.

## Pause to Reflect

The first step toward a high stress IQ is also the most important one: knowing when we are experiencing stress and when we are experiencing vitality. This knowing, or awareness, is the gateway to well-being. Once students have this basic awareness, we can coach them to differentiate the kinds of stress they are experiencing, identify the sources of stress in their lives and in the classroom, and manage these stressors both as individuals and through coregulation with peers. If this sounds like too lofty a goal, don't worry: We will cover how to guide this process in the following chapters.

Take a moment now to reflect on your experience guiding students through the first three learning cycles of the stress-wise framework. What did you learn about your students? Did anything surprise you? What did you learn about yourself in the process? We encourage you to accept Dena Simmons's (2021) invitation to "start a practice of reflecting on [your] identity, positionality, power, and privilege" as they relate to the process of facilitating learning. Doing this will deepen your ability to make space for the diverse experiences your students bring to the table when they feel seen and heard. Are you centering the voices of your students of color? Are you allowing what is real for students to enter the process even if it feels irrelevant to you personally?

Spending some time in reflection will benefit the ongoing work of growing stress intelligence in your classroom. As your awareness of what is working grows, let it guide your way. Feel free to repeat any practice or activity that feels beneficial and effective. Indeed, body-mind-heart practices are *meant* to be repeated. As practitioners and educators, we have repeated some of the same practices daily for decades! Engaging in awareness practices is like brushing your teeth: a nonnegotiable (and refreshing) key to health.

# 3

# Differentiate: The Science of Stress

> **Guiding Question**
> How can educators help students identify the different kinds of stress they are experiencing?

Stress comes in different forms. Short-lived, tolerable stress can be healthy and promote learning, while chronic stress can be debilitating (Jensen, 1998; Liu et al., 2017). Knowing the difference between chronic and acute cycles of stress can make all the difference in how we move through our daily classroom routines. Through the practice of differentiation, we can learn how to mitigate stressful experiences for better outcomes.

Some learners perceive *all* stress as a monster to avoid. For others, it's the opposite: In a culture where being constantly busy is a measure of success, stress can signal effort and progress. Differentiation serves to break down the monolith of stress into a series of manageable parts to allow for the healthiest results.

# Complete Versus Incomplete Stress Cycles

Many of us get an anxious, jittery feeling before speaking in front of a large group as we brace for the audience's judgment. This feeling can indicate the beginning of a positive stress cycle. In our brain, the amygdala sends an alert signal to the hypothalamus, which acts like a command center to the rest of the body via the nervous system. In response, the body releases adrenaline, which leads to a cascade of physiological reactions: increased heart rate and blood pressure, rapid breathing, perspiration, even changes to the digestive system. *Stress is physiological—it is an adaptive state.*

It is also supposed to be a temporary state. The physiological reactions occur so quickly that we may not even notice them. A few seconds into the presentation, we look around and see the caring eyes of our colleagues and realize that we are safe from judgment. We then go on with our presentation with just enough stress to keep us engaged in delivering it without leaving us feeling wiped out afterward. After the presentation, we celebrate by jumping up and down (releasing the stress response physically) and chatting with friends (settling the mind with connection), and we can continue our day with ease. Our dynamic ability to move from a stressed to a non-stressed state creates a healthy rhythm of vitality and natural flux that allows us to thrive. This is an example of a complete stress cycle.

The images in Figure 3.1 (see p. 50) of the complete and incomplete stress cycles, as represented by the Ferris wheel, show the repetitive pattern of stress we can find ourselves caught in. Finding yourself stuck on a Ferris wheel dangling uncomfortably in the air could create a continued stress response. Yet if you are able to come back to the ground and experience safety, you can deactivate a stress response to prevent a chronic state and find equilibrium. Your ability to deactivate, or shake off the stress, enables you to restore and prevent a continued stress response from becoming chronic.

Now consider what would happen if there were an earthquake during the middle of the presentation. The entire audience is asked to seek safety, and after the shaking subsides, everyone returns to their homes.

### Figure 3.1. Complete Versus Incomplete Stress Cycles

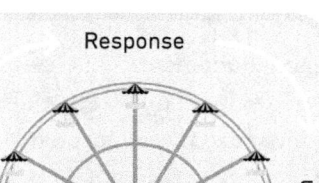

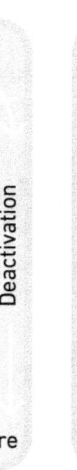
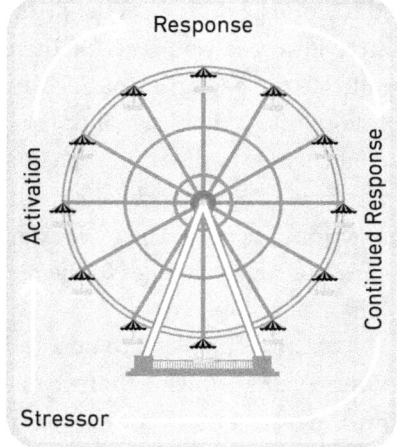

This shock, coupled with our inability to discharge the cascade of physiological stress reactions while feeling isolated and unsafe, may cause us to fall into a longer-term pattern of stress. We may not be able to sleep that night, so we skip breakfast the next morning and opt for a larger cup of coffee, continuing through the day as though nothing happened. A few months later, someone asks us to give another presentation, and suddenly an overwhelming feeling of dread takes over. This is an example of an incomplete stress cycle.

## The Power of a Peaceful Pause

Think of body-mind-heart practices in the classroom as moments of pause from the ceaseless grind of daily life. It is in these pauses that our stress intelligence develops as we access our ability to respond rather than react to stimulus. Habitually overreacting to stressors normalizes and reinforces poor coping skills, creating a culture of distress. If we consistently overreact to events that we have no immediate control over, like traffic or the weather or everyday annoyances like misplacing our keys, we can practice utilizing mindful practice to recenter ourselves, take a pause, and find the space to respond in a calmer and healthier way.

## Perception and Stress

Perception plays a big role in the type of stress we experience. One person's "good stress" is another person's "bad stress." The term *eustress* refers to helpful stress that sharpens our focus, increases motivation, boosts or streamlines performance, and is often experienced with excitement, hope, and enthusiasm, whereas the term *distress* refers to stress that protects us from threat by focusing our faculties only on what's necessary for short-term survival and is often experienced as a feeling of overwhelm, anxiety, and frustration. When we are experiencing eustress, the energy we harness to overcome a stressor is proportionate to our needs, and our sympathetic response is strategically channeled to arrive at solutions. By contrast, when we are in distress, we expend excessive energy and have more trouble finding a solution to our stressor. Knowing and differentiating among these stress types expands our capacity to endure and navigate stress (Damour, 2019).

In large part, whether we experience eustress or distress is determined by our perception of our ability to cope with the demand. In a scenario where the stress event seems like something we can work through successfully (e.g., getting to our next class across campus in under five minutes), we will not overexert ourselves to do so. This "low-stress" experience, or eustress, will require us to exert just enough effort and energy to get through the demanding experience (a quicker pace or a light jog to our destination), complete the stress cycle (getting to class before the bell rings), and resolve back into a baseline level of being—usually a parasympathetic state (sitting at our desk and returning to a regular breathing pattern). However, if that demanding event seems beyond our ability to cope and we don't have the resources to help us feel like we can handle it, it will qualify as a "high-stress" experience, or distress. We'll exert more energy and effort trying to cope with it and the negative emotions it stirs up rather than resolving the demand.

# Learning Cycle 1
# Types of Stress and How Vitality Relates

**Objectives**
- Dispel the notion that all stress is "bad" stress.
- Introduce the stress–vitality spectrum.
- Practice differentiating states of stress in the body and mind.

**Outcomes**
- Students will recognize that stress and vitality are connected.
- Students will be able to detect the kinds of stress they experience.

**Keywords:** *eustress, distress*

## Phase 1.1: Engage. The Stress–Vitality Spectrum

**Timeframe:** 20 minutes

**Class Discussion**

Pose the following prompts and have students respond to each one in "say anything" rounds:

1. Is stress helpful, harmful, or both?
2. Are there different kinds of stress? If so, name them.
3. Is it possible to experience stress and vitality at the same time?

Next, present the stress–vitality spectrum shown in Figure 3.2. Feel free to adapt the language to meet your students where they are.

Using the following prompts, invite students to assess where they land on the spectrum as they reflect on different aspects of their lives. They can draw the spectrum in their journals and mark their locations for each prompt:

- When you are engaged in your favorite activity, where do you land on the spectrum?

**Figure 3.2. The Stress-Vitality Spectrum**

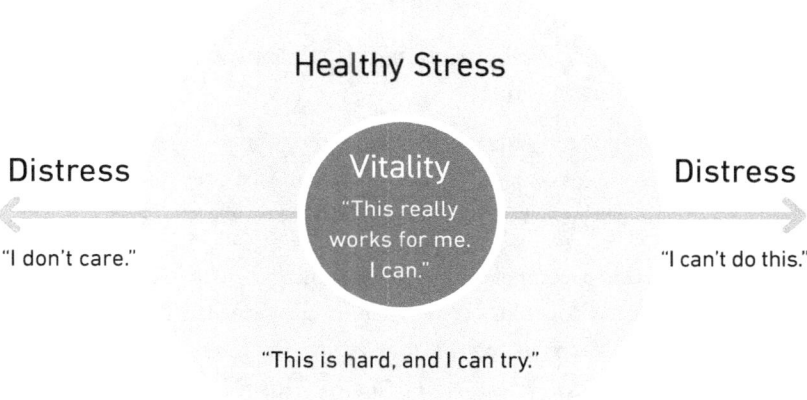

- When you think about your experience with your closest friends or the people you like best, where do you land on the spectrum?
- Thinking about your school experience in general, where do you land on the spectrum?
- Where do you land on the spectrum right now?

To close out this phase, remind students that thinking about stress as part of a spectrum rather than as either "good" or "bad" helps us become more self-aware, and that our attitude toward a stressor has an impact on our ability to cope with it. Just because something feels like it's too hard or insurmountable doesn't mean it will go away, but having awareness that something feels too hard can lead us to ask for help or access another resource to help shift our attitude and get through it in a wise way. This helps us modulate strong emotions and get through challenges in a healthy way. Being stress wise means that we know where we are on the stress spectrum because we're aware of how we feel and therefore don't get stuck outside the "healthy stress" zone for too long. Where stress meets wisdom, vitality can grow.

## Phase 1.2: Explore. Spectrum Situations

**Timeframe:** 20 minutes

**Small-Group Activity**

In small groups, students name situations where they feel like they're in the following zones:

- The vitality zone ("This works for me; I can")
- The healthy stress zone ("This is hard, but I can try")
- The distress zone ("I don't care," "I can't")

When they're done, each group identifies one situation from each zone to share with the whole class. You can also consider the following bonus prompt: "When you're in the distress zone, what is something that can help you go from 'I don't care' or 'I can't' to 'This is hard, but I can try' or 'This works for me; I can'?"

## Phase 1.3: Embody
### Feeling the Difference: Peaceful Poses

**Timeframe:** 5 minutes

**Whole-Group Activity**

Students can sit or stand for this short practice of embodied differentiation. You can use the following script:

> First, make your body be really loose, like a floppy rag doll. Let your head flop over to one side. Slouch. Let your jaw hang open.
>
> Next, tense up your body. Hold your body stiff and rigid. Lift your shoulders up to your ears. Squeeze your lips together. Can you breathe well in this position?
>
> Now, find your comfort zone. Not too loose, not too tight, but just right. In your just-right pose, you'll be able to breathe easier and feel a sense of steadiness in your body, mind, and heart.

## Phase 1.4: Expand. Stress Is Not the Enemy

**Timeframe:** 10 minutes

Write the words *eustress* and *distress* on the board. Explain to students that stress can fall into one of these two categories. Eustress leads to growth, but distress can cause harm. Explain that eustress is helpful "I can" stress, while distress is hurtful "I can't" stress.

**The Sympathetic and Parasympathetic Nervous Systems**

Share the following with students, either by reading it aloud or by paraphrasing.

When we experience stress, the command center of our brain, the hypothalamus, communicates with the rest of the body through the autonomic nervous system, which includes both the sympathetic and parasympathetic nervous systems. When we reflexively move our hand off a hot stove, it's the sympathetic nervous system that makes this reaction possible by flooding the body with energy so that it can respond to danger quickly. Like the gas pedal in a car, our sympathetic response revs us up by changing our physiology so we can move quickly and effectively away from a threat. This function is inherently wise and protects us from danger and possible death.

Of course, if there is a gas pedal, there must also be a brake pedal. That's the parasympathetic nervous system, which helps us to slow down after having been revved up by a stressor. Our body slows down to a rest-and-digest state, redistributing energy so we can complete revitalizing processes like sleeping, eating, resting, and enjoying the company of others.

If the sympathetic nervous system represents the flight part of a flight-or-freeze response, the parasympathetic controls the freeze part, which is something like slamming on the brakes to avoid a collision. Once we feel safe, we can ease off the brakes and begin to move again. Finding a balance between our inner gas and brake pedals is essential to living a stress-wise life. (See Figure 3.3 on page 56 for an illustration of the functions of our sympathetic and parasympathetic nervous systems.)

## Figure 3.3. Sympathetic Versus Parasympathetic Nervous System

| Body-Based Symptoms | Sympathetic Nervous System | Parasympathetic Nervous System |
|---|---|---|
| Pupils | Dilate | Constrict |
| Heart rate | Increases | Is regulated |
| Adrenaline | Is secreted | Leftover is metabolized |
| Saliva (digestion precursor) | Is inhibited | Is stimulated |
| Digestive activity | Is inhibited | Is promoted |
| Sexual arousal | Is inhibited | Is uninhibited |

## Phase 1.5: Express
### "Speed Up or Slow Down" Wisdom Share

**Timeframe:** 10 minutes

Provide students with the following journaling prompts:

- When do you feel the gas pedal being pushed in your life?
- When have you noticed the brakes working?
- What helps you hit the brakes when you need to?

# Learning Cycle 2
# Navigating Different Types of Stress

**Objectives**
- Investigate the impact of stress on learning.
- Practice the technique of pausing mindfully.
- Contemplate ways of knowing when to slow down and when to amplify.
- Know how to differentiate between the self and the experience of stress.

**Outcomes**
- Students will develop regulation skills through enhanced somatic awareness.
- Students will learn how to press pause on purpose.

**Keyword:** *pause*

## Phase 2.1: Engage. The Power of a Pause

**Timeframe:** 5–10 minutes

**Tap and Pause Practice**

This practice works well when you serve as a conductor, leading the changes in intensity and the pauses. Ask students to sit in chairs with their feet on the floor, then follow this script:

> Begin to tap your toes lightly on the floor. Alternate the taps from left to right. Tap at a medium pace. [Students tap for a few seconds.] Now tap very slowly. [They tap for a few seconds again.] Now tap fast; I will count down from three to one. After one, we pause: three [students start tapping], two, one, pause [students stop tapping]. In this pause, simply notice any sensations in your feet. [Pause for 10–15 seconds.]
>
> Now start tapping your heels. Alternate right and left heels, tapping lightly at a medium pace. [Students tap for a few seconds.] Now tap very slowly with a little more force. [Students tap for a few seconds again.] Now tap fast; I will count down from three to one. After one, we pause: three [students start tapping], two, one, pause [students stop tapping]. In this pause, simply notice any sensations in your feet. [Pause for 10–15 seconds.]

Have students repeat the toe taps, conducting shifts in intensity and rhythm. Shift between slow and fast, light and heavy, alternating and synchronized. Play with counting down to pause and the duration of the pauses. Use these gestures for your countdowns: three fingers, two fingers, one finger, fist.

Once students have had some experience with this tap and pause practice, you can recruit a few to lead it. After several rounds, ask students to name anything they noticed during the pauses.

Apply this practice anytime you feel a need for grounding or refocusing.

## Phase 2.2: Explore. The Impact of Stress on Growth

**Timeframe:** 10–20 minutes

**Small-Group Activity**

In small groups, students discuss and take notes on the following questions:

- How does stress motivate your learning?
- Name some scenarios where eustress has had a positive impact on your learning.
- How does stress interfere with your learning?
- Name some scenarios where distress has had a negative impact on your learning.

## Phase 2.3: Embody
### Press Pause: Complete a Stress Cycle

**Timeframe:** 5–10 minutes

Before starting the following practice session, ask students to identify where they find themselves on the stress–vitality spectrum.

**Shake and Drop Practice**

These simple movements can be done seated or standing. Follow this script:

> Shake your hands out as if they are wet. Shake, shake, shake. I will count down from three to one. After I say "one," drop your hands and pause. OK: three, two, one, drop. Pause. Now simply notice what is here in this pause.

Repeat this exercise several times, pausing for a little longer each time. Try to sense how long you can pause before students begin to stir. Let the pauses linger as long as there is a sense of quiet and spaciousness. Invite students to shake out different body parts: head, face, shoulders, hips, legs, feet. You can also use a bell or chime to signify the pause or invite student volunteers to lead the practice.

Following the exercise, lead a short check-in by asking, "What did you notice in the pauses?" As students respond, ask, "Did anyone else notice that?" and "Who noticed something different?" Remember that checking in after body-mind-heart practices is about figuring out what students noticed.

You can apply this practice anytime you feel a need for releasing energy or completing stress cycles.

## Phase 2.4: Expand
### How Do We Know What Speed to Go?

**Timeframe:** 5–15 minutes

Before starting, ask students to identify where they find themselves on the stress–vitality spectrum. Then, guide students through the following contemplation and discussion:

> Have you ever been in a car that felt like it was going too fast? How did you feel in your body when that happened? Imagine that you are driving with someone who suddenly slams on the brakes only to then speed up quickly because they are driving across town in rush hour. What do you notice about this driving style and how it feels in your body? That sensation of feeling on edge or like you're on a roller-coaster is very similar to how we feel when we have not completed a stress cycle. [Guide students to notice their individual responses to being in a car with a driver who slams on the brakes.]
>
> Now imagine you are in a car with someone who is driving too slowly. As you inch your way closer to your destination, you realize that what should've been a 5-minute drive is taking closer to 30 minutes. How does it feel in your body to be in this car? What would you want to happen differently? How would it change your experience? [Guide students to notice their individual responses to being in a car with a driver who's going too slowly.]
>
> Sometimes we need eustress to help us become motivated and move forward in our lives. If we are constantly pressing the brakes or moving too slowly, it becomes hard to accomplish our goals.
>
> How can you use the metaphor of the gas and brake pedal to make different decisions in your life? How do we know the difference between going too fast and going too slow?

## Phase 2.5: Express
### Stress Is Something We Experience, Not Who We Are

**Timeframe:** 10 minutes

**Journaling Prompt**

Provide students with the following journaling prompt:

> Draw a line down the center of a page. At the top of one side of the line, write the heading "Stress I Experience." At the top of the other side, write "My Self."
>
> Under "Stress I Experience," describe the stress you experience. You can list how the stress feels or what you feel stressed about.
>
> Under "My Self," list words or phrases that describe you, your aspirations, or your passions.
>
> Differentiate yourself from the stress you experience. If you'd like, write "I am not the stress I experience" at the bottom of the page.

# Learning Cycle 3
# Putting Stress in Perspective

**Objectives**
- Define resilience as a contributing factor to vitality.
- Boost students' confidence in their ability to cope with stress.
- Explore and learn from regulation in the natural world.

**Outcomes**
- Students will learn to use body-mind-heart practices for self-regulation.
- Students will learn to nurture traits that increase vitality.

**Keywords:** *resilience, regulate*

## Phase 3.1: Engage
### Contemplating Growth and Resilience

**Timeframe:** 15 minutes

**Class Discussion**

Use the following prompts to start a discussion, then write (or recruit a student volunteer to write) students' responses on the board:

- What does a plant need to grow?
- What does every human need to grow?
- Where do we see commonalities? Differences?
- What supports us in meeting our needs?

If it doesn't come up in the responses, define resilience for students as the ability to recover from life's challenges. Ask, "What contributes to your resilience?"

This is a big question, and resilience will be addressed again in subsequent chapters. The goal of asking the question here is simply to bring awareness to students' experiences of resilience. If you wish, you may share this short list of factors that contribute to resilience:

- Feeling connected to loved ones
- Eating healthy foods
- Getting the right amount of sleep
- Spending time in nature
- Creativity, play, and imagination

## Phase 3.2: Explore. Resiliency in the Real World

**Timeframe:** 20 minutes

**Small-Group Activity**

Have students answer the following two questions in small groups:

1. Where can we find examples of resilience in nature?
2. You know what humans need to grow, but what do we need to *thrive*?

When students are finished, give each small group a couple of minutes to share its findings with the whole group. After each group shares, invite feedback on commonalities and differences across group responses.

## Phase 3.3: Embody. Guided Meditation for Resiliency

**Timeframe:** 10–15 minutes

Guide students through the following mindful breathing and reflection practice:

> First, pause to notice the parts of your body that are in connection with the floor or chair. Next, close or halfway close your eyes. Now, begin to notice your breath. For a few moments, simply observe each inhale and exhale. Slowly begin to deepen each inhale, as though the breath brings a sense of softness to the inside of your body. Imagine each inhale is like a river gently carving its way through dense earth. Feel how your body can expand from inside during the inhale. Begin to lengthen each exhale, softening muscular tension in your shoulders, neck, and face. Keep breathing and softening for one minute.
>
> Now, think about how resilient your body is. Staying soft and breathing fully, remember a time when your physical body accidentally got hurt. Maybe you had a fall and twisted an ankle or cut yourself while cooking. Or maybe you can think of a time when you were able to fully heal from being sick. How does your body know how to heal? Where does your resilience come from?
>
> Finally, has there been a time in your life when you were able to overcome a challenge that seemed overwhelming at first? Imagine that your deep breathing can guide you to your own resilience and help you self-regulate during stressful times. Where do you find resilience within yourself?
>
> Slowly bring your awareness back to the room and the space around you. Take a few moments to look around and reorient yourself to the outside world.

Allow students five minutes to share their findings in dyads (pairs) or triads (groups of three).

## Phase 3.4: Expand. Stress Is Only Part of the Picture

**Timeframe:** 5 minutes

**Materials:** posterboard or chart paper

Read the following script to help students understand the interaction of stress, well-being, and vitality. If you want to share your own version, please do! Feel free to get creative:

> Our bodies are dynamic, meaning that they are changing and growing in any given moment and are impacted by many things. Similarly, our well-being is influenced by a myriad of factors like the environment, sociopolitical contexts, and how much we eat, sleep, and feel connected to friends and family.
>
> Likewise, we can see that in a garden there is a cycle of stress, well-being, and vitality that grows in stages. In the stress stage, soil is amended with compost as it navigates the challenge of creating microbes that sustain its health. As the compost does this, the soil begins to regulate water, cycle nutrients, and provide the foundation for plant life. As the soil becomes resilient, seeds are planted to begin their process of germination. The seeds incubate in the soil's thriving microbiome, taking in the nutrients and water that they need to grow. At this stage of well-being, the seeds sprout and begin their journey from the soil to the outside world. This stage is full of energy, fast change, and growth. However, a stressor like a rainstorm or a pest could negatively impact the sprout, restraining it from growing further.
>
> Different crops require different conditions to flourish. For example, broccoli grows better in cold weather, while tomatoes grow better in hot weather. Some crops, like tomatoes and basil, grow best when planted with a companion; others, like mint, are so resilient they can grow throughout the year with very little intervention.
>
> If the sprout withstands adversity at this stage, it moves into a state of vitality. This indicates that the plant is thriving. It receives nourishment from the soil, sun, and water. It is

> protected from extreme weather and pests. The plant is harvested when it reaches its peak or goes to seed to create a new generation of plants.
>
> Human beings also cycle through these stages of stress, well-being, and vitality. These stages are always changing, and becoming aware of our individual needs as we grow can help us to withstand the stress of growing. Just like plants in a garden, sometimes we're caught in a rainstorm that we can't escape.
>
> What nutrients do you need to better withstand the challenges of life?

As students share their responses, list them on a poster or paper to keep as a reminder for the class.

## Phase 3.5: Express. Vitality and Stress Go Together

**Timeframe:** 5–15 minutes

The following activity will deepen students' understanding of their own bodies in relation to the stress, well-being, and vitality cycle.

Have students draw an outline of a body and follow prompts to fill in or journal responses to the prompt (see Figure 3.4 for an example). Read the following prompts, or ask a volunteer from the class to read them aloud:

- Imagine your body as a garden full of vitality. What traits do you want to grow in your garden?
- Where do you want to plant the seeds of these traits?
- What other traits can you cultivate here?
- What nutrients are needed to grow these traits?
- How do the traits support one another?
- Are there any elements like water or sunshine that help these traits to grow?
- What stressors will these traits have to overcome to sprout?
- How can you create safety and protection so these traits can come to their full expression of vitality?

## Figure 3.4. The Body as a Garden of Vitality

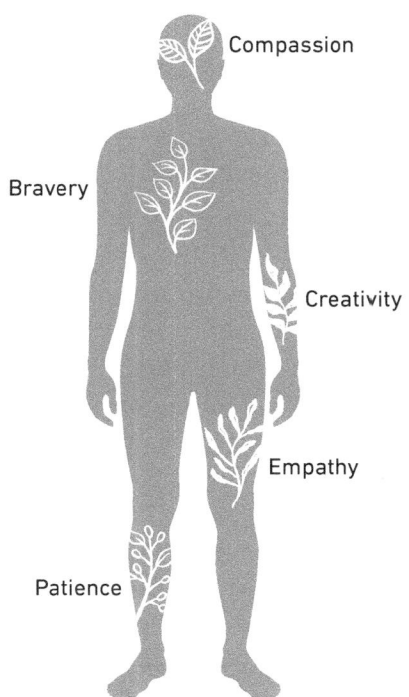

# Learning Cycle 4: Stress Is Part of a Cycle

**Objectives**
- Portray stress and vitality as natural and cyclical.
- Illustrate the dynamism of a stress cycle.
- Differentiate between complete and incomplete stress cycles.

**Outcomes**
- Students will accept that stress is natural.
- Students will trust in the body's magnificent mechanisms for coping.
- Students will be aware of their potential to flourish through stress intelligence.

**Keywords:** *stress cycle, chronic, acute*

## Phase 4.1: Engage. Cycles and Seasons of Growth

**Timeframe:** 20 minutes

Read the following script aloud, ask for a student volunteer to read it aloud, or paraphrase it in your own words.

> As the seasons change throughout the year, we cycle through phases of stress and vitality in the natural world. In fact, even our moods and physical functioning are impacted by the change of the seasons in nature. Just like the seasons changing, we too have different needs depending upon our external circumstances.
>
> Through the changes in the seasons, trees can undergo drastic changes in their appearance and needs. Trees in the springtime tend to have abundant leaves and can grow a lot during this time as they reap the benefits of hydration from the prior winter season. In the summer, trees can reach their full potential, perhaps even showcasing blossoms. As the fall settles in, leaves begin to change color and fall to the ground. Some trees in the wintertime become fully bare, even surprising us with their ability to grow back in winter. Let's discuss how these seasonal changes affect us.

Use the following prompts to guide a discussion with students.

- What do you notice about the changes in the seasons?
- How does the weather affect the trees?
- Which season makes you most think of vitality?
- Which season looks like the most stress?
- What would happen if the seasons did not change?

Guide the discussion by helping students see that each stage is necessary to trees' growth. Even when a tree is bare, it is preparing for the next cycle of growth. Without shedding and wintering, the tree would not complete a full seasonal cycle. And just like us, the tree is capable of weathering great storms that make it stronger and more resilient.

Have students reflect on the following prompts and respond in their journals:

- Can you relate to the cycles the tree is going through?
- Have you ever experienced a time in your life that felt like a long winter?
- How about a new beginning that felt like spring?
- What is your favorite season? What can you learn about this season and your relationship with stress?

## Phase 4.2: Explore. When the Cycle Gets Stuck

**Timeframe:** 20 minutes

> **From Niki's Classroom**
>
> When Niki taught graduating seniors from a medical magnet high school program, she had them self-assess their energy levels at the start of every day to decide what type of practice they would do: mecitation, a more athletic yoga, breathwork, or guided visualization. Alexa consistently came to Niki's biweekly sessions on the brink of collapse and usually fell asleep if they practiced being in repose quietly together.
>
> Beyond the obvious rigor of her scholastic responsibilities, Niki didn't know what could be causing Alexa's exhaustion. She read Alexa's stress symptoms as best she could and relied on mindful practices to help restore balance to her and the other students who were under so much pressure to do well in school.
>
> Near the end of the semester, Alexa raised her hand.
>
> "I don't have a stomachache today," she announced. "Almost every day, my stomach hurts. It makes it hard for me to concentrate or eat. But today something is different. I think this class has something to do with it."

We know that digestion is negatively impacted by both acute and chronic stress (Konturek et al., 2011). To get this feedback from Alexa was not only a relief, but also evidence that her ongoing state of distress was likely allayed by the mindful practices Niki had been incorporating in class.

Share this quote from Emily and Amelia Nagoski's 2020 book *Burnout: The Secret to Unlocking the Stress Cycle*:

> The good news is that stress is not the problem. It's how we deal with stress—not what causes it—that releases the stress, completes the cycle, and, ultimately, keeps us from burning out. You can't control every external stressor that comes your way. The goal isn't to live in a state of perpetual balance and peace and calm; the goal is to move through stress to calm, so that you're ready for the next stressor, and to move from effort to rest and back again. (p. 27)

Explain to students that when we are stuck in "on" mode, it can be hard for our bodies to complete a stress cycle. A "Go! Go! Go!" mentality taxes our bodies and minds and leaves us without an opportunity to reset. Just like our electronic devices, we need downtime to recharge. We also need motivation to get us moving again so we can complete a stress cycle.

Have students partner up. Encourage them to listen to one another mindfully, with compassion and curiosity, as they share their responses to the following prompts:

- How do you know when you're feeling stuck in "on" mode?
- What activities pump the brakes for you?
- How can you help point out to a friend or family member that they might be stuck in "on" mode?
- Have you ever felt like you were stuck without moving forward?
- If so, what motivated you to get moving again? What makes you go?

## Phase 4.3: Embody. Ocean of Tranquility Meditation

**Timeframe:** 5 minutes or more

Guide students through this mindful practice:

> Let's begin by finding a comfortable sitting or lying down position, with eyes closed or gently open. Begin to notice sensations that are present in your body. As you start to slow down, soften your shoulders down and away from the ears. Allow your jaw to soften. Let the muscles around your eyes start to relax. As you settle here,

notice where your body holds stress, maybe in the form of tension or tightness.

With your next exhale, imagine that your tension starts to soften and drift away, like a wave receding back into the vast ocean. Each wave carries fear, worry, anger, or a feeling that takes away from your happiness. With an inhale, imagine the cool and tranquil waters of the ocean washing your body with ease and relaxation.

Each inhale brings peace, calm, joy, and even a sense of excitement.

Each exhale is an opportunity to shed some of the stress.

As you experience your breath flowing in and out of the ocean of tranquility, notice what sensations change in your body. Do you notice any more relaxation? [Pause here until students begin to stir or there is a sense of being ready to come back as a group.]

Feel free to stay with any quality of relaxation you've tapped into as you bring your attention back into the room and our shared space.

We can take a few moments to share aloud how this activity was for you. What does relaxation feel like in your body? What does stress feel like in your body? How can you remember the sensation of relaxation?

## Phase 4.4: Expand
### Riding the Stress Cycle: Short and Long Rides

**Timeframe:** 15 minutes

Show students the image of the stress cycle Ferris wheel in Figure 3.1 (p. 50). You can also recreate the image or ask students to do so. Then, follow this script:

In an acute stress cycle, we ride through different physical and mental states as though we're on a Ferris wheel. When we sense a stressor, like giving a presentation or fighting with a parent, our brains get the signal to get on that Ferris wheel. We experience changes in our body: Our heart races and our body temperature and digestion change. Stress hormones like adrenaline get released so we can respond to the stressor quickly, just like when we're at the top of a Ferris wheel and we experience butterflies in our belly or feel the need to scream. We use this uptick in energy to take action against the stressor—also known as *mobilizing*. Then, like reaching the end of the Ferris wheel ride, our "rest and digest" system returns us to homeostasis.

Sometimes, if we don't properly discharge all the energy that comes with experiencing stress, or if we freeze instead of mobilizing, we can get stuck on the stress Ferris wheel—a state of chronic stress. This can cause us to feel scattered or unmotivated, like we want to hide, or hypervigilant. We may startle easily or feel like we are moving too fast and constantly on the go.

Have you ever felt this way? What helps you hit the brakes when you are moving too fast? What helps you get energized when you feel stuck?

Bring awareness to the idea that slowing down, though challenging, can be important for completing the stress cycle, just as sometimes getting active and moving is what helps us get back to our balanced selves.

Next time you become aware of heightened stress in your classroom, ask students to consider what they might need to find balance. Would a short quiet pause be helpful? Or a brisk walk for a few minutes? Giving students a choice to practice completing stress cycles throughout the week, especially in conjunction with known stressors, can contribute to more sustained balance.

## Phase 4.5: Express. Stress Cycle Check-In

**Timeframe:** 10 minutes

Issue the following survey in Google Forms or another convenient format for collecting responses:

1. Can stress sometimes help you achieve your goals? ___Yes ___ No
2. Are you interested in knowing the difference between stress that helps you and stress that gets in your way? ___Yes ___ No
3. An example of healthy stress is _____.

4. To be resilient, I can (select all that apply):
   \_\_ Connect with loved ones
   \_\_ Eat a bunch of sugar
   \_\_ Get a good amount of sleep
   \_\_ Spend time in nature
   \_\_ Watch TV all night
   \_\_ Create, play, and imagine
5. List some activities that you find hard but rewarding:

   - _____
   - _____
   - _____
   - _____

After students complete the survey, check in about their responses. Questions 1, 3, and 4 will show a baseline of understanding. If needed, clarify with students that stress *can* help us achieve goals and invite them to share examples of healthy stress. Question 2 provides a simple check-in on students' openness and willingness to learn about stress. This information may be helpful for forming small groups in the future. Be sure to support students who are struggling to engage by placing them in groups with members who are interested in the stress-wise process. If students select "eat a bunch of sugar" or "watch TV all night" for question 4, you might point out that although sugar and television are not inherently bad, they are not likely to contribute to resilience, especially in excess. Throughout the stress-wise process, use the responses to question 5 as examples to remind students that hard things can be rewarding. If a student names baseball as something they find hard but rewarding, encourage them to approach assignments with the same spirit they use to approach baseball. Remind students that the spirit they bring has a direct impact on their experience.

# Reframing Stress Helps to Change How We See It

In the hustle and bustle of school life, it's common for students to function under high levels of stress without exploring the science behind it.

Demystifying stress can empower students to take a more active role in their personal and collective health. Simply knowing there are different kinds of stress gives your students an upper hand in growing into stress-intelligent learners.

We know that time is at a premium in all classrooms and hope you will begin to see the benefits of taking some time to incorporate stress-wise practices into the daily grind. Every classroom is different, and we've seen an array of outcomes from implementing stress-wise praxis. Some classes experience benefits immediately, whereas others take more time to integrate the practices.

This is a good juncture to reflect on your unique classrooms process. Are you seeing some of your students engaging and participating wholeheartedly in stress-wise praxis? If so, how can you harness their brilliance to inspire others to engage? For students who are resistant or less interested, how can you shift gears to promote more engagement? Can you try a different time of day or week to lead activities and practices, or check in with students about their impressions of the process?

We encourage using the stress–vitality spectrum for regular check-ins with students and anytime they need help differentiating eustress from distress. Don't worry if every student is not showing a high level of interest yet. Giving students the opportunity to consider their own states of being is meaningful, even (or perhaps especially) for those still struggling to make a connection to themselves.

Finally, we want to acknowledge you for devoting time and energy to supporting your students' well-being. Equipping students with a space to talk about stress helps to normalize the fact that every person at every age experiences it, shining a light on our common humanity. Holding space in school to develop a life skill like differentiating stressors and knowing how to pause before reacting can contribute to health for a lifetime. We can't help but wonder how our own lives would have been different if our schoolteachers had taught us some of this in our formal education. We applaud you!

# 4

# Identify: Sources of Stress, Coping, and Vitality

**Guiding Question**

How can educators help students discover the sources of stress in their lives and learn to manage their own stress?

At this point in the stress-wise process, students know more about what stress and vitality are and have learned some basics about how stress functions in their bodies, brains, and minds. This chapter focuses on discovering the origins of stress in students' lives and ways to cope that optimize students' health and wellness as learners.

Developing an awareness of our stressors is a critical step in the process of demystifying stress and acts as a precursor to mindful and effective stress management. When students can clearly see the sources of stress, they are better able to make informed choices about the activities and people they engage with. Of course, a prolonged focus on stressors can be taxing on students' minds and nervous systems, so mindful practices are integrated throughout each activity in the stress-wise framework for balance, recovery, and nurturing of coping skills.

When we ask teenage students to name the main stressors in their lives, we hear a litany of common responses: school, family, friends, their own bodies, substance abuse, money, work. Teens often name macrosystem stressors as well, such as policing, generational poverty, racism, politics, discrimination, food insecurity, and homelessness. Social and environmental justice issues burden adolescents with stress that is not being adequately addressed.

The teenage brain is restructuring itself in a way that amplifies everything, so it's no wonder many teens feel their stress levels are out of their control, leading them to the "I don't care" stage. The buildup of stress, lack of mental health care in many schools and communities, and a dearth of effective coping skills have resulted in a tragic increase in teen suicides, suicide attempts, and acts of self-harm. According to the National Alliance on Mental Illness, 50 percent of all lifetime mental illness begins by age 14, and one in six youth ages 6–17 experience a mental health disorder each year. Compared with their peers, these students are three times more likely to repeat a grade, and high school students with persistent depression are more than twice as likely to drop out of school. Following the 2020 COVID-19 pandemic, there was a 31 percent increase in mental health–related emergency department visits for people ages 12–17 (National Alliance on Mental Illness, 2022). The risk in guiding students to identify stressors is that they can feel overpowered by the wayward world. To avoid this, we highlight their potential to thrive at every turn. Whenever we ask students to think about the stressors in their lives, we also ask them to identify where they have power, control, and choice.

## From Coping to Thriving

By unpacking the origins of their stress, students learn that the most stressful relationships and activities also provide us with the most life-giving and rewarding outcomes. For example, teens often name extracurricular activities like sports as major sources of stress. A stress-wise lens helps them to see that the stress they experience is balanced by the results.

The stress-wise framework empowers youth to make conscious choices about who and what to prioritize in their lives, to easily identify what types of stress are productive and what types are destructive, and whether their chosen coping strategies lead to more freedom or yet more intense stress.

# Identifying Stress and Supporting Students Through It

When students begin to feel more trust and safety in their learning environments, they may become more willing to share their experiences with you and the class—and you need to be ready to provide them with the necessary support.

**From Abby's Classroom**

Jocelyn, an 8th grader, shared with her class that her main stressor was being "low-key" targeted by two different gangs in her neighborhood. As a biracial person, Jocelyn did not feel safe walking down her street because members of both rival gangs, divided by race, saw her as on the other side. Jocelyn dealt with the fallout of this distress daily at school. Jocelyn tended to be withdrawn, but after sharing this stressful experience with her peers, she was noticeably relieved and better able to participate in class.

Though her classmates' compassion and support certainly helped bolster Jocelyn's ability to cope with her reality, Abby felt she needed further support. As a white-bodied educator, Abby felt her ability to guide this student was limited and that it was important for Jocelyn to be connected with a person who could help her find strategies and solutions.

Fortunately, the school employed a biracial restorative justice facilitator who was able to help Jocelyn tremendously. Together, Jocelyn, Abby, and the facilitator made a plan for Jocelyn to be dropped off at the house of a friend with whom she could walk to school in the mornings. This solution did not change the tragedy of racial violence in Jocelyn's neighborhood, but it dramatically shifted her day-to-day experience at school, giving her better access to her own brilliance and potential. Jocelyn was eventually able to channel her traumatic experience into a poem expressing how she felt when she was being targeted, her newfound sense of support and safety, and her desire for a post-racial world in which all people belong regardless of skin color. She created an audio version of her poem that was included in a schoolwide presentation. This experience boosted Jocelyn's confidence tremendously. She transitioned from essentially hiding alone in corners (of classrooms, the cafeteria, and the recess yard) to actively participating in classroom discussions and accepting social invitations from peers. Attempting to be invisible had been a coping strategy for Jocelyn. Once other students understood her experience, they naturally started to recruit her into social activities.

Stress-wise praxis recognizes that students' personal lives don't stop affecting them when they're inside the school gates. Schools can become safer and more satisfying for students, as Jocelyn's school did for her, when we acknowledge not just students' academic learning capacities but also their experiences as a whole (Suldo et al., 2008).

# Learning Cycle 1
# Identifying Sources of Vitality

**Objectives**
- Differentiate coping outcomes.
- Cogenerate coping strategies.
- Investigate how food, sleep, and exercise contribute to well-being.
- Inspire creative visioning of needs for navigating stress.

**Outcomes**
- Students are empowered to enact helpful ways of coping with daily stress.
- Students' personal and collective vitality is elevated due to self-appreciation and the appreciation of others.

**Keywords:** *appreciation, coping, needs*

## Phase 1.1: Engage. Practice Appreciation

**Timeframe:** 20 minutes

**Class Discussion**

Share the following questions and statements with students as starting points for class discussion:

- What do you appreciate about our class as a whole?
- Every day will bring both stress and gifts. We can find balance by practicing appreciation.
- Appreciating each other is one way to cope with daily stress.
- What does coping mean?
- What are some other ways that we cope with stress?

## Phase 1.2: Explore. Coping Mechanism Show-and-Tell

**Timeframe:** 20 minutes

**Materials:** box or envelope

Invite students to think about what helps them cope in stressful situations—things like watching television, eating a snack, doing yoga, or going for a run. Like stress, coping comes in different forms, some helpful and some not. Ask each student to make a list of 5 to 10 helpful coping strategies in their journals. Then have them write down their favorite coping skill on a small piece of paper. Pass around a box or an envelope to collect all the coping skill ideas, and then ask a student to read them aloud.

**Optional creative application:** If using a box, bring it to the center of the room. Ask students to help decorate it with any creative items available. In this box, students will be invited to put coping skills they use that would be helpful to share with others. Keep the coping toolbox in the classroom for students to continue adding to it.

## Phase 1.3: Embody
### Guided Meditation for Self-Appreciation

**Timeframe:** 10 minutes

Use the following script with your class.

Find a comfortable position for your body. Take a few moments to settle into yourself. [Pause.]

Soften your eyes. Lower your gaze or close your eyes. [Pause.]

Draw your attention to the space around you. Notice the sounds you hear around you. [Pause.]

Feel the air touching your skin. Notice the temperature of the air. [Pause.]

Feel your body in connection with the earth. [Pause.]

Feel free to sway side to side or forward and back if that helps you soothe.

Bring your awareness to your inner body. Notice any sensations. [Pause.]

Can you feel your breath flowing in your body?

Can you find one part of your body to soften? [Pause.]

Think of one thing you appreciate about yourself right now. [Pause.]

Think about some of the ways you help other people in your daily life. Think about the ways you let your loved ones know you love them. [Pause.]

Can you offer love and appreciation to yourself? Infuse your breath with appreciation.

Breathe as much love as you can into your body. [Pause.]

Let your breath relax and go back to normal. Feel your heartbeat. Feel your feet on the ground and the support beneath you. Notice the space around you. Slowly lift your gaze or open your eyes. Take a few moments to bring your awareness fully back to the room.

When you find yourself in a challenging situation, remember that appreciating and loving yourself can help you cope and thrive.

## Phase 1.4: Expand. Identifying Daily Supports

**Timeframe:** 20 minutes

Read aloud the following script, call on a student to read it aloud, or paraphrase it in your own words.

There are three pillars of health that nurture our mental and physical well-being: sleep, food, and exercise. When these pillars are in balance, we become better able to cope with stressors in our lives. Adequate sleep helps us to rest and recover from stress, making us more resilient to the troubles of our days. Getting nourishment and nutrition from the foods we eat is essential to our stress response. When we eat whole foods on a regular schedule, it gives our body the strength and immunity it needs to withstand adversity. Similarly, discharging stress through movement or exercise is one of the most practical tools for stress modulation. Having regular movement as a part of your routine is integral to balancing stress and vitality.

Discuss the following questions as a whole class, or break the class into small groups to discuss one or two questions each.
- What foods give you sustained energy?
- How much sleep makes you feel ready to take on the day?
- What is your favorite type of movement? Is it ever hard to get motivated?
- What obstacles make it hard to get enough sleep? What supports you in getting a good night's sleep?

## Phase 1.5: Express. Stress Assistant Visualization

**Timeframe:** 20 minutes

Use the following script with your class.

Pause to bring your awareness to the base of your body. Feel the ground and chair beneath you, supporting you. Relax your hands. Soften your face and steady your gaze.

Now, imagine you are creating a flyer requesting an assistant who will help you deal with all the stressors in your life. What are your most outstanding needs? What kinds of skills will your assistant need to bring to the job? What type of personality would you like this assistant to have?

Try to visualize your flyer. What colors will you use? Will you include any images? Try to imagine your whole flyer at once. Then, let the image dissolve as you bring your awareness back to your physical foundation. Feel your feet on the ground. Notice your breathing. Slowly bring your awareness back to the room and people around you.

**Creative application:** Students sketch or digitally create the flyers they envisioned. Flyers should specify the students' most outstanding needs, the skills required for the job, and desired personality traits.

**Alternative activity:** Students record the needs, skills, and traits they previously identified in their journals. Encourage them to think of their own minds as their trusty assistants. Over time, they can cultivate the skills or personality traits they named in their job descriptions.

# Learning Cycle 2
# Sources of Strength and Wisdom

**Objectives**
- Ascertain for which stressors students have control and agency.
- Establish anchors to assist with adaptive coping.
- Consider the role of nonviolence in stress intelligence.
- Document ways to cocreate a caring classroom environment.

**Outcomes**
- Students will be able to ground and stabilize themselves using creatively applied body-mind-heart practices.
- Students will gain awareness of human connection as a resource for well-being.

**Keywords:** *overwhelm, anchor, common humanity*

**From Abby's Classroom**

The "ocean of overwhelm" is a metaphor I've used for decades with adolescent students. Teens identify with the sense of expansive, all-permeating stress that the ocean imagery evokes—the feeling that their stress is too big to overcome. By acknowledging that life can sometimes feel like an ocean of overwhelming feelings, we normalize stress in a way that helps students know they are not alone in their experience.

For many years, I offered teens an opportunity to visualize their own boat for navigating the seas of change. We focused on finding balance in the boat. A month into the COVID-19 school closures of 2020, the "ocean" had become so choppy that our boat imagery was not promoting the feelings of safety and belonging it once had. To help students feel more grounded, I switched to having them visualize a lighthouse. As one 16-year-old student expressed, "When I tried to find my foundation like a lighthouse, I felt stronger—like I have a place to be so I'm not just floating around."

## Phase 2.1: Engage. Weathering the Storms of Change

**Timeframe:** 20 minutes

1. **Check-in prompt.** Ask students if they ever feel that life is overwhelming, as if they are swimming in an ocean of overwhelm. Invite students to share thoughts on what being overwhelmed feels like.
2. **Brainstorm.** Students make a "word storm" on a page in their journal answering the question "Where does my stress come from?" Ask them to write the sources of stress in their lives all over the page—a storm of stressors. Notice when the writing begins to dwindle, then move on to the next step.
3. **Flip for control.** Students review their word storm and circle stressors over which they have some control and choice. Then, they flip the page over and only record the circled items. Remind students that an important part of being stress wise is to focus on the sources of stress we can control. Although we can be aware of all sources of stress, to keep from getting overwhelmed, we need to tap into our power and choose which stressors to focus on.

4. **Add anchors.** Remind students that they also have wisdom shifts, coping mechanisms, and body-mind-heart practices to use as anchors. Ask them to recall some of these anchors from previous LCs or to look back through their journals for reminders. Have them add at least one anchor for every stressor they circled in their word storm.

Once the four steps are complete, guide students through the following practice to complete the activity.

**Peace Pause Practice** (2–3 minutes)
Follow this script with your class:

> Bring your awareness to your own space. Notice the space around your body. Enjoy a few deep breaths.
>
> Now, check in with yourself. Notice any signs of stress in your body, mind, or heart and offer yourself a little break. Can you find a little bit of ease in the middle of your stress? [Pause.]
>
> Now, bring your awareness to any part of you that feels strong or alive. Maybe you can feel your heart pumping. Notice that even during stressful times, our hearts continue to beat and keep us alive. Notice the life force moving through your body. [Pause for 10 or more seconds.]
>
> Slowly bring your awareness back to the space around you now. Bring your strength back with you and into your day. Notice any subtle changes in the room as you bring your awareness back to being in the group.

# Phase 2.2: Explore
## An Umbrella for Us All: Common Humanity Exercise

**Timeframe:** 5–10 minutes

Have students gather in a group circle and imagine that the center of the circle is covered by a large umbrella. As you read the prompts below aloud, anyone who answers yes steps forward and under the umbrella. After each prompt, allow a moment for students to look around and see who stepped under the umbrella before resetting the group circle and moving on to the next one.

The prompts are as follows:

- If you have ever eaten broccoli, step in.
- If you didn't get enough sleep last night, step in.
- If you are hungry, step in.
- If you have a sibling, step in.
- If you love watching horror movies, step in.
- If you are experiencing stress in your life, step in.
- If you've ever felt sad, step in.
- If you enjoy spending time with your friends, step in.

Ask students if there are any prompts they would like to add. When the activity settles down, invite students to share their experiences. Remind them that our common humanity helps us weather the storm of stress more easily.

## Phase 2.3: Embody
### A Lighthouse in the Storm Meditation

**Timeframe:** 15–20 minutes

**Materials:** video at www.youtube.com/@StressWisePractices-wo3kv

### Cultivating Relevance

Remind students that awareness is like a flashlight in a dark forest: It can help them find direction when they feel lost, avoid obstacles in their path, and bring out the details of what was once unseen.

As a precursor to this body-mind-heart practice, acknowledge to students that developing awareness about the sources of stress in their lives can feel overwhelming at first. Everyone has stress storms to weather. Encourage students to feel self-compassion since they are doing their best to cope with multiple stressors per day.

Follow the link above to play the audio practice or read from the script in the following section, then proceed with the activity that follows.

### Be a Lighthouse

Prior to facilitating this mindful practice, be sure all students are familiar with what lighthouses and beacons are. If lighthouses are not common in your area, consider presenting an image of one before doing this practice.

Follow this script with your class:

> For this practice, sit as tall as you can in your seat. Place both feet on the floor and find your ground. Relax your hands on your desk. Steady your gaze in one direction. [Pause.]
>
> Feel the strength in the core of your body. Lengthen your whole spine, reaching your upper body toward the ceiling. [Pause.]
>
> Imagine that you are as strong and mighty as a lighthouse, able to weather the storms in your life. Feel your solid foundation through your feet and seat, keeping your structure sound and steady. [Pause.]
>
> Use your awareness, like a light, to find the strength and power in your inner body. [Pause.]
>
> Now, imagine you can utilize your awareness like a beacon from a lighthouse to see through the storms around you. Follow your awareness around your whole body, bringing a sense of clarity and warmth to yourself. [Pause.]
>
> Take a moment to acknowledge your strength and perseverance and know that your strength can grow even as the stress of life gets bigger. [Pause.]
>
> Start to bring your awareness back to the solid floor and chair now. Slowly guide your attention back to the room around you. Take a few moments to stretch or stand up to land back in this room. [Pause.]

Ask students to name times and situations wherein they might call on the lighthouse visualization to help them feel stable and grounded.

## Phase 2.4: Expand
### Roots of Safety: Creating a Stress-Wise Classroom

**Timeframe:** 15–20 minutes

**Materials (optional):** posterboard or chart paper, pens or pencils

Write the word *ahimsa* on the board. Ask if anyone knows the meaning or the translation from Sanskrit to English or any other languages students may speak.

Inform students that *ahimsa* is often translated from Sanskrit as "non-harming" or "nonviolence." Ahimsa was a key tenet of Gandhi's nonviolent liberation movement. Committing to not harming ourselves or others is a fundamental step in creating a stress-wise classroom because it creates the roots of safety that are essential for students to grow. Non-harming is a practice that begins inside us and expands outward into our relationships, societies, and systems.

Share this quote from former U.S. Surgeon General Vivek Murthy with students: "What can we do in our lives, through the decisions we make, the choices we make, to tip the scales in the world away from fear and toward love?" (Tippett, 2021).

Ask students to name ways the whole class can work together to create a safer, more caring classroom environment for everyone. Here are some ideas to get you started:

- Shift to curiosity during conflicts.
- Listen to bodily cues.
- Assume the good in people.

Then, choose one of the following:

- Create a shared digital document for students to add their responses.
- Invite students to write responses on a poster or chart paper.
- Solicit anonymous responses from students, record them in a chosen format, and post them, physically or digitally.

## Phase 2.5: Express
### Harmless Helper Journal Prompt

**Timeframe:** 5–10 minutes

**Journaling Prompts**

Ask students to answer these prompts in their journals:

- Who embodies nonviolence to you?
- Is there someone in your life who serves as a lighthouse beacon for you?
- Likewise, have you been a lighthouse beacon for someone in your life?

# Learning Cycle 3
# Internal Resource Discovery

**Objectives**
- Deconstruct the perception that stress is a monolithic problem.
- Research how food, sleep, and exercise affect stress and vitality.
- Urge students to recognize moments of relative peace as an important counterbalance to stress awareness.

**Outcomes**
- Students will learn to respond to stressors with appropriate intensity.
- Students will purposefully detect and affirm safety.

**Keyword:** *neuroception*

## Phase 3.1: Engage. Sizing Up Stress

**Timeframe:** 10–15 minutes

**Check-In Prompt**

Ask students, "Since we brainstormed sources of stress in your life, have you noticed any other sources to add?" Then, follow these steps:

1. Give students a couple of minutes to review their word storms from the previous learning cycle and make any additions or changes.
2. Ask students to look for strong connections between their word storm responses. For example, if they cite homework as a main source of stress, they may look for other stressors on the page that are related, such as "being tired," "annoying siblings," or "too busy." Students then draw lines in their journals connecting the related stressors.
3. In some cases, stressors may be so closely connected that they can be merged into a bigger topic. For example, if a student has identified both "waking up" and "being tired" as stressors, they might choose to create an umbrella topic for "sleep." Encourage students to look for umbrella topics.

4. Students look for the big, main stressors and circle them. Next, they seek out medium-sized stressors and underline them. Finally, they place a star or hashtag beside the stressors they perceive as small.
5. Students turn their journals horizontally and create five columns labeled Major Stressors, Medium Stressors, Small Stuff, Anchors, and Needs (see Figure 4.1), then transfer the data from their word storms and the flyer from Phase 1.5 in Learning Cycle 1 (see p. 79) to the table.

Figure 4.1. Stressor Inventory

| Major Stressors | Medium Stressors | Small Stuff | Anchors | Needs |
|---|---|---|---|---|
| | | | | |
| | | | | |
| | | | | |
| | | | | |

Here are some optional deeper dives for discussion:
- Can you identify any of these stressors as a catalyst for change in your life?
- Can you imagine some of the "small stuff" falling off the list as your stress intelligence grows?

## Phase 3.2: Explore
### Three Pillars of Wellness to Help Recover from Stress

**Timeframe:** 20 minutes

In this activity, students explore three pillars that help the body and mind heal from chronic stress: food, sleep, and exercise.

1. Form three groups. Assign each group a pillar: food, sleep, or exercise.
2. Groups discuss how their assigned pillar impacts stress and vitality.
3. After a short discussion, students create an illustration, infographic, poem, or sketch that explains why our relationship to food, sleep, or exercise is important to managing stress and increasing vitality.
4. Each group reports back to the whole class.

## Phase 3.3: Embody
### Bridge of Self-Awareness Visualization

**Timeframe:** 10–20 minutes

Use the following script with your class.

> Sit or stand in a comfortable position. Press your feet down firmly to the floor. Feel the weight of your body in your feet. Place one hand on the top of your head. Press your head up into your hand, sending the crown of your head upward. Now, relax your arms and hands in the position that feels easiest to you. Steady your focus in one direction below the horizon or softly close your eyes. Bring attention to the cycles of breath in your body. Explore to find an anchor for your attention in your body, where you feel your breath. Allow your attention to hover gently around your anchor spot without too much effort in your mind. Enjoy a few quiet moments here, gently guiding your attention back to your anchor spot when you become aware that your mind has wandered. [Pause for 10–20 seconds.]
>
> Now, imagine that you are standing on one side of a river looking toward the bank on the other side. The river can be as wide or narrow as you want it to be. Pretend that the bank you stand on represents your current coping skills. Feel the solid ground beneath you that holds the structure through which the river flows. The bank on the other side of the river represents the needs you have already named and charted.
>
> Take your time imagining a bridge across the river. Visualize the bridge in any way you want. It can be a mighty architectural

feat or a simple beam. Take your time and "see" as many details as you can. [Pause for a minute or longer if students appear engaged.]

Decide if you want to imagine yourself walking across your bridge now or if you prefer to wait until another time. It's up to you. [Pause.] When you are ready, allow the imagery to fade and guide your attention back to the floor beneath you here in the room and become more aware of the people around you.

Invite students to share about their bridges either to the whole group or in pairs. You may also encourage students to draw or write about their bridge.

## Phase 3.4: Expand. The Science of Feeling Safe

**Timeframe:** 10–15 minutes

Write the word *neuroception* on the board.

Ask students if they remember what *interoception* and *exteroception* are. If not, remind them that, simply put, interoception detects internal signals like hunger, thirst, and heart rate, whereas exteroception takes in signals from outside the body such as sights, textures, tastes, sounds, and smells and helps us know our place in a space. Then, follow this script with the class:

> Let's focus on how we can grow our ability to find more peace in our lives. Over the next week, try to notice when you feel safe. This feeling may occur in a particular place or with certain people. Safety is different for all of us. The experiment is to become aware of feeling safe and breathe into that feeling. Try to enjoy those moments when life feels mostly OK and you find a sense of peace in yourself.
>
> Some of us have to work at finding peace. If you desire more peace in your life, start to look for places and people that feel safe to you. As much as possible, spend more time in and with those places and people. When you do find a moment of peace, make a note in your mind—something like "Peace is here" or "I feel safe."

## Phase 3.5: Express
### Identifying Internal Resources Check-In

**Timeframe:** 10 minutes

Issue the following survey in Google Forms or another convenient format for collecting responses.

1. Does knowing the sources of vitality in your life help you deal with stress? ___Yes ___ No
2. Are you curious to know more about how to cope well with stress? ___Yes ___ No
3. Fill in the blanks: I feel a sense of belonging in spaces that are _____ and with people who are _____.
4. We can create a more peaceful classroom environment by (select all that apply):
   ___ Assuming the good in each other
   ___ Making space for all voices to be heard
   ___ Ignoring people with whom we disagree
   ___ Taking responsibility for our own feelings
   ___ Gossiping about each other
5. List three sources of stress that are common to many people:
   a. _____
   b. _____
   c. _____

Invite students who answered yes to question 1 to share why they think knowing the sources of vitality in their lives helps them deal with stress. This will help students connect the dots between vitality and well-being. Question 2 is your baseline check for willingness to learn. Notice if students are fluctuating in their openness throughout this process. If a student who has been interested seems to be losing interest, consider asking them why. On the other hand, if a student who has been disengaged is showing newfound interest, a small celebration may be in order; something as simple as a high-five or note of acknowledgment can meaningfully boost student confidence. If necessary, invite dialogue on why gossiping and ignoring people can be detrimental to a peaceful classroom environment. Consider sharing responses to question 5 anonymously to deepen students' experience of common humanity—one of the most effective ways to relieve the feeling that the weight of the world is on our shoulders. Remind students that stress is natural and common to every living being.

We are now midway through the stress-wise process. While Chapters 2 and 3 primed students by introducing them to awareness and the science of stress, the learning cycles in this chapter have brought students into a deeper awareness of the specific sources of stress in their own lives. In the three chapters that follow, we cover how to make wise choices, resourcing, and coregulation.

This midway point is a perfect time to reflect on which stress-wise practices have been most effective for your class. Is there anything you would like to do differently next time you lead the first three learning cycles? Are there any body-mind-heart practices you plan to carry forward into your teaching practice? Going forward, we encourage you to look for opportunities to bring the learning cycles alive by infusing your own creativity into the process. The more you bring yourself to the process, the more willing students will be to show up whole as well.

# 5

# Discern: Making Wise Choices

*Wellness is not a state of being—it's a state of action. It is the freedom to oscillate through the cycles of being human. Real-world wellness is messy, complicated, and not always accessible. If you sometimes feel overwhelmed and exhausted, that doesn't mean you're doing it wrong; it just means you're moving through the process. Grant your body permission to be imperfect and listen to your own experience.*

—Emily and Amelia Nagoski

> **Guiding Question**
> How can educators help students develop the skills necessary for healthy decision making?

Discernment is key to responsible decision making. Mindful practices help students develop the ability to respond rather than react to stimuli, including stress. The learning cycles in this chapter give students opportunities to practice responsive discernment in tricky situations. Sensory experiences are included to help students direct their attention and develop concentration during stressful situations. Through guided visualization, students will use their imaginations to explore their power to choose to modulate out of distress states and into relaxation states.

Not every classroom moment will be the epitome of vitality, but we can often find at least a seed of vitality to nurture in the challenging moments. From that seed, a voice of wisdom helps guide us to choices that continue to promote vitality and help us navigate stress efficiently. This voice of wisdom knows what life is like when we feel at ease, present, aware, and able to settle into a state of calm. Sometimes we listen to this voice, sometimes we don't. Our work is to help strengthen awareness of that voice so that we have more opportunities to listen to it and then act based on what we hear.

### From Niki's Classroom

I begin class sessions with a question to gauge how students are feeling and what level of vitality we have to work with. Near the end of a semester in 2018, I asked, "How many of you got enough sleep last night that you woke up today feeling refreshed and ready to go?" No one raised their hand. "How many of you didn't get enough sleep last night and know because you woke up today feeling tired or didn't have the energy to feel your best?" All 17 students confirmed that they were getting far less than the recommended 8–10 hours each night. Half had jobs outside school, and all were enrolled in numerous extracurricular activities.

Knowing that stress was a major factor in students' lives, we started each session with a mindful self-evaluation examining the quality of sleep they got, their current mood, how much energy they had for physical activity, and whether they needed mental focus to get work done or mental relief to find repose. Across the sessions, the great majority of students consistently needed rest through restorative yoga and guided meditation. The option for a more vigorous physical practice was available to them each week, and given their young age, a more athletic session could be presumed to be the next best choice for them. But offering students the agency to follow their internal sense of wisdom and take a more holistic view of their lives beyond the classroom suited their needs in those moments at the end of the school day.

Normalizing relaxation as a skillset to be used for health and success rather than something to be earned allowed this ambitious and burned-out group of young adults the reprieve they needed to find stress wisdom. As one student shared with me in the second week of our program, "I slept through the night for the first time in two weeks yesterday. I feel amazing today!"

## Reaction Versus Response

Whether we *respond* or *react* to stress helps determine the type of stress we experience. Practicing discernment can help us respond to stressors mindfully rather than react out of unconscious habit.

For example, imagine you're late for an appointment for some reason beyond your control. During your journey, you are anxious and annoyed; your breath is shallow, and your gut and shoulders are clenched. You might be worried about what other people will think of you or about disappointing a colleague. When you reach your destination with a well-rehearsed apology, you discover that the event has been delayed by unrelated circumstances. You are now free to release the pressure that has built up, sigh, and maybe even chuckle. If only you had known the event was delayed, you could have enjoyed your trip instead of worrying the whole time.

Now imagine what would have changed if you had tried to enjoy your journey despite the stressors. What if you had been able to determine a useful amount of alertness to get you safely to your destination close to the appointed time while still maintaining a sense of well-being? If you had properly calibrated your body's response, you'd be free to breathe your way through the experience, maybe even enjoying a stress-relieving activity along the way.

What if you were able to accept your late arrival? How might it feel in your body and mind to offer yourself some compassion, knowing that you were not to blame for the unforeseen delays?

Apply this lens to a personal situation when you recognized, in hindsight, that your reaction to a stressor exacerbated the situation. Ask yourself whether the level of stress you experienced was necessary and useful or if your reaction to the stress amplified an already challenging situation. If the latter is true, how could you have dealt with the situation differently in order to prioritize your well-being?

Discernment allows us to calibrate how we spend our energy and maintain a sense of well-being throughout a stressful experience. How intensely we respond to stress is something we can learn to modulate through practices that allow us to mindfully sense states of equanimity as well as by shifting from sympathetic to parasympathetic responses. Discovering our unique "stress symptoms" contributes to our self-awareness and allows us to mindfully choose which symptoms to treat when we are truly overreacting.

# Learning Cycle 1
# Using Somatic Awareness and Joy to Respond More Thoughtfully to Stress

**Objectives**
- Explore the physical, mental, and emotional signals involved in wise decision making.
- Develop the meaning of discernment.
- Contextualize somatic awareness as a tool for applying discernment to decision making.

**Outcomes**
- Students will learn to utilize somatic awareness when making difficult decisions.
- Students will connect to joy as a fundamental aspect of well-being.

**Keyword:** *discernment*

## Phases 1.1 and 1.2: Engage and Explore
### Signals from Our Body, Mind, and Heart

**Timeframe:** 20–30 minutes

In Chapter 2, Phase 3.2 (p. 41), students journaled about the physical, mental, and emotional signals they experience in states of both stress and vitality. You may prompt them to reference those notes as you complete this exercise.

**Class Discussion**

Start with the following script:

> How many of us have been in a situation where our heart says one thing and our head says another? Raise your hand if you have ever felt yourself being pulled in different directions. Can anyone give an example of a time when you needed to make a decision but felt unsure, and what physical, mental, or emotional signals you experienced during that time of indecision?

Then, share the following "traffic lights" rubric with students:

- Green light means "go" or "yes."
- Yellow light means "slow down" or "pause."
- Red light means "stop" or "no."

Next, ask students these questions:

- What green lights might you detect in your body, mind, or heart letting you know the choice is "go" or "yes"?
- What yellow lights might you detect letting you know the choice is "slow down" or "pause"?
- What red lights might you detect clearly letting you know the choice is "stop" or "no"?

**Small-Group Activity**

Students form small groups to discuss and list signals they can look for in their bodies, minds, and hearts when making tough decisions:

- What signs make you go? (green lights)
- What signs give you pause? (yellow lights)
- What signs stop you in your tracks? (red lights)

When they're done, invite students to share highlights or "aha" moments with the whole group. To close the discussion, remind students that feeling pulled in different directions is normal and that the process of developing stress intelligence can help us tap into our power of discernment to choose wisely.

## Phase 1.3: Embody. Inner Wisdom Body Scan

**Timeframe:** 5–20 minutes

**Materials:** video at www.youtube.com/@StressWisePractices-wo3kv

Follow the link to play the audio practice or read from the following script, then proceed with the activity that follows.

**Body-Mind-Heart Integration Practice**

Follow this script with the whole class:

> Find a comfortable position for your body right now. Bring your awareness toward yourself. Feel the solid ground beneath you. Find your center. Soften your gaze. Notice your breathing.
>
> Notice your breath moving in your body. Can you sense your breath in your chest or belly? Let's move our mind around the body, checking in with different parts to see how we feel right now. Let's start at the top. Place your awareness at the top of your head. Visualize or sense the top of your head. Can you feel it without using your hands to touch it? Now bring awareness to your eyes. How do your eyes feel? Bring awareness to your cheeks. Notice your cheeks. Your nose. Your jaw. Bring gentle awareness to your shoulders. Notice where they are—no need to move them; let them rest. Now bring your attention to your upper back. Sense your back muscles, your spine. Let your back rest into the floor. Notice your hips. How do your hips feel right now? Listen to your body. Bring awareness down through your legs. Observe how your legs are without needing to move them, let yourself rest—just use your mind. Bring awareness to your feet. Feel your feet, each one. Now shift attention to your hands. Where are they? What are they touching? Simply observe this. There's nothing to do but notice. Now sense your arms. How are your arms right now? Bring your

awareness to your chest. Can you feel your breath inside your chest? Finally, rest your awareness on your belly. Can you feel your breath moving your belly?

Allow your attention to wander through your body toward a place that feels tight or dense. Notice if this place can release even a little bit with a gentle effort. There is no need to force it. Simply be curious. Look for one more part of your body that feels tense. Will that part easily release a bit if you watch for a moment?

Now bring your attention to any part of you that feels relaxed and free. Perhaps you will find a sense of relaxation in the soles of your feet or the palms of your hands, or maybe there is a feeling of openness in your heart or mind. If you find it, stay with that feeling for a few moments, or keep looking gently for a place of relaxation within yourself.

Let yourself slow down even more. Let go of looking for any particular signs now. Simply allow yourself to pause and breathe for a few more moments. Know that you can slow down anytime to check in with yourself and notice the wise signs your body and mind are sending you.

Can you recall a situation where your head said one thing and your heart said another, and looking back, you know you made the wise choice? What helped you to make that choice? [Pause.]

Begin to bring your awareness back into the space around you. Take your time to lift your gaze and notice the room and people in it.

Next, ask students these questions:

- Did you notice any tight places? Did they loosen at all as you noticed them?
- How about any open and relaxed feelings?
- When do you think you might use a practice like this in your life?
- Were you able to recall a situation where your head said one thing and your heart said another, and looking back, you know you made the wise choice? What helped you to make that choice?

## Phase 1.4: Expand. Signals from Our Food

**Timeframe:** 10 minutes

Read the following script aloud, ask a student to read it aloud, or paraphrase it in your own words.

> Wisdom allows us to discern between choices that help us in the long term and choices that bring temporary relief. One way we practice discernment regularly is through our food choices. When we eat foods that are healthy for our bodies, we feel energized. When we eat foods that aren't as nutritious, we feel sleepy after eating. How we feel 30 to 60 minutes after eating indicates how much, if at all, the food is nourishing our body. Each of us has unique nutritional needs, and staying aware of how the food we eat makes us feel helps us make wise choices about what nourishes our body and mind.

Ask students to jot down what they ate yesterday and then answer these questions:

- Which of these foods gave you energy?
- Which made you tired or lethargic?
- Which had no noticeable effect?

Now read aloud the following script:

> Identifying and heeding the different signals our bodies send to help us make decisions develops our somatic awareness. I invite you to ask the questions above when making decisions about food so you can not only continue becoming stress wise but also become food wise.

## Phase 1.5: Express. Signs of Joy on Display

**Timeframe:** 5–20 minutes

**Materials (optional):** card stock or cardboard, markers, scrap paper, or other art materials

**Artwork Activity**

Wise teachers know that joy indicates a healthy path. For this activity, have students think about what brings them joy—people, places, activities, foods, dreams, and anything else that comes to mind. Then, individually or in pairs, students make signs illustrating these sources of joy and post them in places where they might inspire joy in others.

**Alternative journaling prompt:** Write or draw about what brings you joy.

# Learning Cycle 2
# Refining Our Wisdom
# Through Intentional Choices

**Objectives**
- Tap into the power of choice through storytelling.
- Create inquiry-based strategies to bridge uncertainty and fortitude.
- Explore the Window of Well-Being (WOW) as a tool to strengthen discernment.

**Outcomes**
- Students will gain the courage to shift states through the power of choice.
- Students will learn how to widen their WOW.

**Keywords:** *choice, fortitude, Window of Well-Being*

## Phase 2.1: Engage. Choosing Our Wisest Response

**Timeframe:** 5–10 minutes

Invite students to rest in a comfortable position where they can mindfully listen to the following parable:

Once upon a time, a daughter complained to her father that her life was miserable. "I'm tired of constantly struggling all the time and not getting anywhere," she complained. "It seems like life is just one problem after another."

Her father took her to the kitchen, where he filled three pots with water and set them to boil. Once the water was boiling, he placed potatoes in one pot, eggs in the second, and ground coffee beans in the third. He let everything boil without saying a word to his daughter, who moaned with impatience.

After 20 minutes, the father turned off the burners. He took the potatoes and eggs out of their pots and placed them in bowls. He filtered the coffee from the grounds and poured the coffee in a mug. Turning to his daughter he asked, "What do you see?"

"Potatoes, eggs, and coffee," she replied.

"Look closer," he said, "and touch the potatoes."

She did and noted that they were soft.

He then asked her to take an egg and break it. After pulling off the shell, she observed the hard-boiled egg.

Finally, he asked her to sip the coffee. Its rich aroma and warmth brought a smile to her face.

"Father, what does this mean?" she asked.

He explained that the potatoes, eggs, and coffee beans had each faced the same adversity—boiling water—but each one reacted differently. The potato went in strong, hard, and unrelenting, but in boiling water, it became tender and weak. The egg was fragile, with only the thin outer shell protecting its liquid interior, but in the boiling water, the inside of the egg became hard. But the ground coffee beans were unique: They changed the *water*, creating something new.

"So, which are you?" the father asked his daughter. "When you're in a pot of adversity, how do you respond? Like a potato, an egg, or coffee grounds?"

Say to students, "In life, things happen around us and things happen to us, but the thing that truly matters is what happens within us. We have the power to choose new ways of responding to life in any moment. So, which one do you tend to be—potato, egg, or coffee?"

Give students time to contemplate their answers. Allow them to share their responses aloud, then ask this follow-up question: "How do you know when your response is not ideal? What signals do you get from your body or in your mind that let you know your reaction isn't the wisest, and what can you do differently to respond better?"

> **From Niki's Classroom**
>
> Leading a group of students through this activity, I had assumed that most students would say they want to be like coffee. To my joyful surprise, that wasn't the case. One student shared: "I'm really sensitive like my dad, so I'm most like an egg. That looks like me getting very quiet during a confrontation and then escaping to my room so I don't have to show my emotions to anyone. I want to be more vulnerable and in touch with my feelings, so I want to be more like the potato and soften up when things get challenging."
>
> In a contemplative and compassionate teaching paradigm, there are no right or wrong answers. I asked students what being more like a potato might look like, and here's how one student responded: "That could look like me being able to say, 'I'm feeling scared right now and need time to process that. I'm going to take a break in my room, but I'll come back and finish the conversation in an hour.'"

Prompt students to write "Potato, Egg, Coffee" in their journals as a reminder that they have multiple ways of responding to adversity.

## Phase 2.2: Explore. Asking Better Questions

**Timeframe:** 20 minutes

Review the "yellow light" signals from Phase 1.1. These are signs to pause and ask questions that can prompt creative problem solving and help us move forward with more focus.

**Small-Group Activity**

In small groups, students discuss the following prompts:

- What kinds of questions can you ask yourself when you are unsure about a decision?
- What kinds of questions can create a bridge from uncertainty to clarity?
- In situations where certainty is impossible, how can you deal with uncertainty?

Invite groups to share their responses with the whole class.

## Phase 2.3: Embody. Clear View Visualization

**Timeframe:** 10 minutes

Invite students to find a comfortable position for a guided visualization practice, then follow this script:

> Imagine that you are lying down in a comfortable bed gazing out of a big window. You notice the outline of rolling hills in the distance and a few clouds in the blue sky moving slowly with the wind. Just outside the window, there is an expansive field with room to roam. Butterflies and hummingbirds fly around freely, stopping to take in nectar from colorful flowers. As you listen to birds chirping, you take a slow exhale, letting all the tension drift away. Maybe you take a sip of delicious mint tea while savoring the smell and noticing the warmth in your hands. What else do you notice as you imagine looking out this window?

After a few minutes of contemplation, invite students to share what they noticed with the class.

## Phase 2.4: Expand
### Introduction to Our Window of Well-Being

**Timeframe:** 10 minutes

Daniel J. Siegel (1999), UCLA professor and advocate for adolescent health, uses the "Window of Tolerance" to illustrate different states of stress and coping. Our "Window of Well-Being" (WOW) is inspired by Dr. Siegel's work and his major contributions to the field of mindful awareness.

Present the WOW graphic in Figure 5.1 to students.

**Figure 5.1. WOW Graphic**

**Too Much Energy**

"I'm all over the place and having a hard time slowing down enough to see through my window."

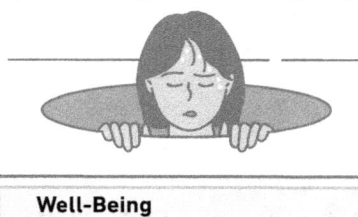

**Well-Being**

"I can see what's good in life even when stress is present."

**Lack of Energy**

"It's hard to see through the window because I'm feeling stuck here on the floor."

Be sure to emphasize that being above or below the window are not choices we make but, rather, states that take over our systems. Where we *do* have choice and power is in becoming aware of the state we're in. Once we do this, we can begin to find our way back to our WOW.

Sometimes our window is wide open, and we can feel the breeze flowing through it. Other times it is barely open, and every little thing feels irritating. When we notice how the window makes us feel, we can ask ourselves better questions to widen our WOW: Do I need a break from whatever I'm doing? Deep breaths outside? A talk with a friend? A glass of water? A nap? Any of these resources can help widen our WOW. As our stress-wise capabilities grow, our Window of Well-Being opens wider, allowing us to withstand challenges without being catapulted above or sunken below the window.

## Phase 2.5: Express
### Finding Our Window of Well-Being

**Timeframe:** 10–20 minutes

**Movement Practice**

Follow this script with students:

> Pause to notice your energy level right now. Where are you in relation to your Window of Well-Being?
>
> In your day-to-day life, what brings you back into your window? Are there specific activities, people, or places that help you? For a few moments, bring those centering activities, people, or places into your awareness.
>
> During this simple movement practice, we will bring our awareness and energy deliberately to the center of our bodies.
>
> Sit or stand in a comfortable position. With an inhale, stretch both arms out to the sides and then overhead in a circle pattern toward the ceiling. On your exhale, bring your hands down to rest on your heart center or on your belly.
>
> We'll repeat this movement 10 to 12 times. Inhaling, stretch your arms up to the sky. Exhaling, place your hands on the center of your body. Move slowly with ease.

Count out the first five or six repetitions, then let students practice on their own count for the next few. Once everyone has completed their rounds, pause for a few moments, then ask students to consider where they are in relation to their WOW.

Next, ask students to create a visual or written description of their WOW. Ask them what they see when they look outside their window and what they see when they look into it from the outside.

# Learning Cycle 3
# Acting Wisely with the World

**Objectives**
- Strengthen connections to the voice of wisdom through relational activities and knowledge of gut brain.
- Distinguish between tolerable and intolerable stress.
- Generate a list of helpers.

**Outcomes**
- Students will be able to confidently make decisions and set boundaries.
- Students will know how to send soothing safety signals to the brain.

**Keywords:** *voice of wisdom, boundaries, enteric nervous system*

## Phase 3.1: Engage. Getting to Know Our Voice of Wisdom

**Timeframe:** 10–15 minutes

**Class Discussion**

Ask students what they think the term *voice of wisdom* means. After giving them time to think about the question, follow or adapt this script with your class:

> Can you think of a time when you've ignored your inner voice of wisdom? Maybe by gossiping about a friend, telling a fib, or skipping brushing your teeth? Each of us has a voice of wisdom that

helps us to make better decisions. Sometimes we listen to this voice of wisdom, and sometimes we ignore it.

Our voice of wisdom can be influenced by role models in our lives who encourage us to make wiser decisions. Do you know anyone who represents a voice of wisdom for you?

What are some times in your life when you have listened to your inner voice of wisdom, or VOW?

Where does your VOW come from? Does it live in your body, mind, or heart? What about all three?

What or who else might influence this voice?

When is your voice of wisdom loudest?

Are there any practices in your life where your voice of wisdom could use some strengthening, like staying up too late, eating too many sweets, or procrastinating on homework? What stress-wise practices could you use to help make your VOW louder and easier to connect with in these more challenging moments?

## Phase 3.2: Explore. Setting Boundaries and Finding Help

**Timeframe:** 20 minutes

**Class Discussion**

Ask students these questions and discuss:

- How do you know the difference between tolerable and intolerable stress?
- What are some examples of tolerable stress?
- What happens when you experience intolerable stress?

Follow or adapt this script with your class:

When we bring our voices of wisdom together, we can learn and share advice that we may not have otherwise considered. Our voices of wisdom can help us support one another to become stronger together.

Knowing whom you can go to for help strengthening your voice of wisdom is hugely helpful when life feels challenging, as is learning to set boundaries by saying no. Saying no can be intimidating at first, but it becomes very powerful once we practice it and feel the positive effects of greater strength, relief, and clarity. Start by setting small boundaries, like saying no to food you don't like, staying up too late, or a friend with whom you disagree. We get better at what we practice, so over time it can become easier to say no to bigger stressors in your life—which ultimately helps you say yes to self-compassion and self-respect.

**Small-Group Activity**

Students discuss the following prompts and record any responses that they feel are empowering:

- What are some examples of tolerable stress you shared earlier?
- How can your voice of wisdom help during stressful times?
- Is there someone you feel safe sharing your stressors with?
- Is it OK to ask them for help?
- Are there any small changes you can make to help during the time of stress?
- Are there places in your life where you can practice saying no?
- What makes it easier for you to hear your voice of wisdom?

**Follow-Up Class Discussion**

Invite students to share back any elements they found empowering. Then, help the class generate a list of people they can ask for help when stress becomes intolerable. Consider listing the following resources:

- You
- Other teachers
- Coaches
- Family members
- Community members
- Mentors
- Spiritual or religious leaders
- School counselors, psychologists, and support staff
- Friends
- Parents of friends
- The National Suicide Prevention Lifeline: 800-273-8255
- The Trevor Project: 866-4-U-TREVOR

- Teen Line: 310-855-4673
- GLBT National Youth Talkline: 800-246-7743
- DeHQ LGBTQ Helpline for South Asians: 908-367-3374
- Trans Lifeline: 877-565-8860
- JED: jedfoundation.org
- Mental Health First Aid: mentalhealthfirstaid.org/mental-health-resources
- Strong 365: strong365.org
- National Queer and Trans Therapist of Color Network: nqttcn.com/en
- The Steve Fund: stevefund.org/backtoschool

## Phase 3.3: Embody. Simple Self-Soothing Practices

**Timeframe:** 10 minutes

Follow this script with the class:

> When we are aware that our stress level is too high, we can send a soothing message from our body to our brain to help lower it and return to our WOW. Just as remembering something stressful or scary can cause physical symptoms that mimic stress, our minds can also create body-based experiences of calm and joy.

Then share the following simple practices with students that help them tell their brain, "I'm OK. I'm safe right now. Let's switch gears and relax."

### Infinity Tips

1. Squeeze and release your shoulders a few times.
2. Roll and stretch your neck a few times, right and left. Loosen up the place where your head and neck meet.
3. Imagine the tip of your nose is a felt-tip marker. Begin to draw a tiny infinity symbol with the tip of your nose. Start slow and small. Keep your gaze soft and relaxed.
4. Widen the symbol, making your movements fluid and smooth.
5. Slowly make the movements small again, then pause.
6. Enjoy a few deep breaths and think, "This too shall pass."

**Soothing Sway**

1. Seated or standing, find your anchor points with the ground or chair. Feel the support and strength beneath you.
2. Soften your gaze.
3. Find the center of your body. From your center, begin to sway slowly and subtly side to side. Find a rhythm that feels soothing to you.
4. Shift the sway to forward and back, finding your own pace.
5. Choose the direction that feels most soothing to practice swaying for a few minutes.
6. After a minute, come back to stillness, quietly noticing how you feel and if your mind and emotions have started to calm down.

## Phase 3.4: Expand. Our Gut Instinct Is Intelligent

**Timeframe:** 10 minutes

**Materials:** Figures 5.2 and 5.3

Share the images in Figures 5.2 and 5.3 (see pp. 111–112) and the following information with students. Consider inviting a student volunteer to read the following script aloud:

> There is a very intelligent part of our bodies called the enteric nervous system, or the "gut-brain." If you've ever had butterflies in your stomach or just had a "gut feeling" about a situation, then you've interacted with your gut-brain! The gut-brain resides in your entire digestive system and has 500 million neurons, which are like communication messengers (Johns Hopkins Medicine, 2021). They communicate messages through chemical and electrical impulses that act like our internal sensory organs. Externally, our eyes, ears, nose, mouth, and skin help us perceive the world around us. Inside, our gut does the job of our sensory organs to let us know if there is anything we need to be aware of.
>
> For example, bacteria might come in through our food, alerting our gut that something is not right. The gut-brain then communicates this signal to the larger brain through a really long

and important nerve called the vagus nerve (Krowiak, 2021). Our gut-brain sends signals up to the larger brain 10 times more often than the other way around. When the gut-brain sends signals of distress to the larger brain, it can result in us experiencing anxiety, depression, and other changes in our mood because the gut-brain can set off the alarm of our sympathetic stress response. When our body is in a state of fight-or-flight, it is common for the digestive process to be negatively affected, and vice versa: our state of mind is negatively affected when our digestive process is disrupted. This is why it is so important for us to take care of our digestive system by eating foods that nourish us and give us lots of vitality.

As a discussion prompt, ask students if they can remember a time when they listened to their gut-brain.

### Figure 5.2. Microbiome

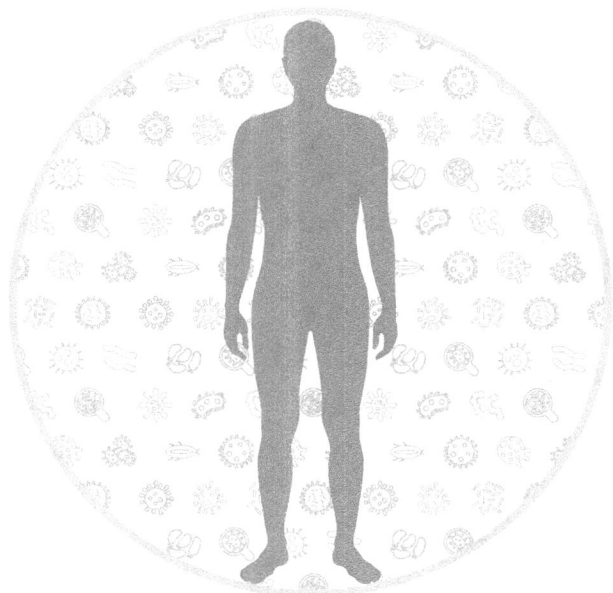

### Figure 5.3. Gut-Brain Axis

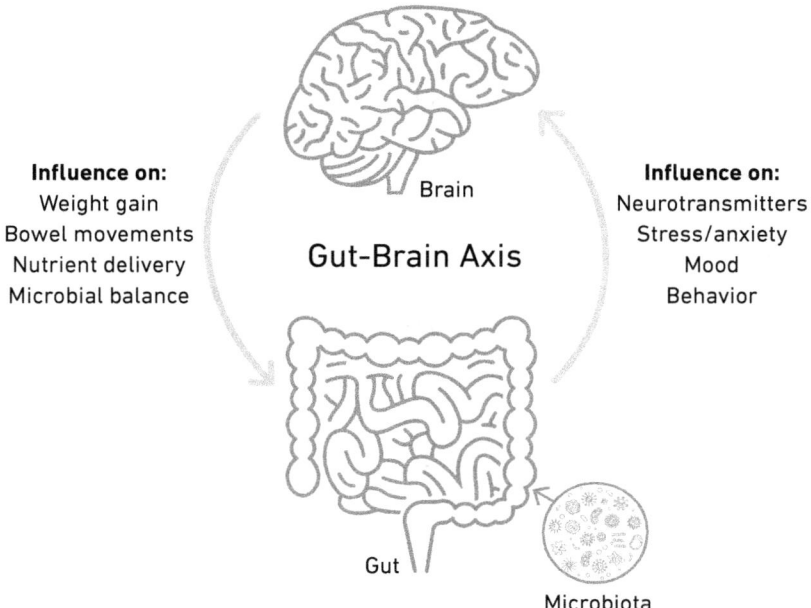

### From Anjali's Classroom

When students learn about the gut-brain connection, they are often astonished to find that there are millions of neurons in their digestion that have an effect on their mood. In fact, there are as many neurons in our gut as there are in the brains of five cats. When I ask students how smart their cats are, they generally respond with "Pretty darn smart, Miss." When they think about not one but five of these "brains" in their digestive tracts, they often feel grossed out and shocked, but also inspired. With this information, students begin to understand the importance of the gut-brain and are more willing to listen to the butterflies in their bellies to choose foods that feel empowering rather than restrictive.

## Phase 3.5: Express. Stress-Wise Check-In

**Timeframe:** 10 minutes

**Student Survey**

1. Do you notice that your mind and body send conflicting messages? ___Yes ___ No
2. If you answered yes to the first question, do you know some ways to manage that feeling or get back to a feeling of safety and wisdom? ___Yes ___ No
3. Complete this sentence: "One way I can send a safety signal to my brain is to _____."
4. Having talked about boundaries and when and whom to ask for help, do you feel more confident setting boundaries with others or asking for help when you need it? ___Yes ___ No
5. Is there anything you would like me to know about your experience with stress-wise praxis? _____
   _____
   _____

6. Is there anything you wish your classmates would understand better?
   _____
   _____
   _____

   Would you like me to share this information anonymously? ___Yes ___ No

**Next Steps**

- Make time for a post-survey check-in. Remind students that conflicting messages from the body and mind are normal, but being *aware* of the conflict is extraordinary and a sign of stress intelligence.
- Take note of responses to question 3 and integrate the practices into your classroom when appropriate.
- Use students' feedback to reinforce stress-wise practices in your classroom and point out opportunities for them that they may not be able to detect in the moment.
- Acknowledge any honest feedback to question 5, showing your willingness to accept students as they are without taking their

experiences personally. Doing this builds trust, the foundation of healthy student-teacher relationships.
- Consider how to effectively share any feedback from question 6 with the class. For some classes, simply reading the feedback aloud can be effective, while other class dynamics are better suited for a more reflective process. One option is to send all students an email containing the collective feedback and giving them time to process it. Students may ask clarifying questions that you can invite further feedback about, either in the moment or anonymously later on.

The learning cycles in this chapter are meant to guide students toward using their inner voice of wisdom as a powerful decision-making tool. Undoubtedly, some of your students were already in touch with this voice, and others are still wondering what "voice of wisdom" means as a concept. Not to worry, as this is lifelong work. Eventually, your students will experience their inner VOW and have you to thank for revealing the power and value of pausing to listen.

This voice of wisdom is not some random cognitive murmuring but grounded in the intelligence of the body itself. Each time we engage in practices that strengthen the body-mind connection, we increase our ability to use our VOW when making decisions.

We encourage you to use your own voice of wisdom to discern your classroom's most effective way forward with stress-wise work. Reflect on these questions:

- Which activities and practices have worked best for your class?
- What is the most valuable thing you've learned about stress intelligence so far?
- Have you experienced any frustrations or surprises in your journey so far?
- Which activities will you carry forward, replicate, or leave behind?

We hope this chapter on discernment has equipped you with knowledge, experience, and wisdom to remind yourself and your students that it's possible to make wise choices even when life feels overwhelming and messy.

# 6

# Resource: Building a Healthy Relationship with Stress

**Guiding Question**

What practices can educators integrate into their classrooms daily to nurture stress IQ in students?

This chapter explores one of the most practical dimensions of stress intelligence: the dynamic art of resourcing—that is, the ways we discharge, recharge, and renew when faced with stress. Regular resourcing assists the completion of stress cycles.

Fundamental techniques like taking short movement breaks to discharge the physiological build-up of stress or mindful breathing to switch from a sympathetic to a parasympathetic response and topics like compassion and self-compassion address the multifaceted body-mind-heart complex, acknowledging students as whole persons.

Knowing how to set and reset boundaries is a lifelong practice vital to the practice of resourcing ourselves. The boundaries we learn to set within the classroom will change over time, just as they will within our social, professional, and personal ecosystems—and they have a domino effect: Setting boundaries around the time we spend on our devices before bed affects how restful our sleep is, for example, and taking a "brain break" during eustress activities can ensure we prepare for a final exam or major performance. Reminding students that repose is a form of boundary setting can empower them to break from the norm of incessant productivity. Breathing techniques and somatic practices throughout this book help introduce students to the experience of repose and what it means to take resting breaks in an intentional and conscious way. As we continue to reframe stress as a continuum to navigate rather than a monolith to overcome, students gain skills that they can immediately apply both inside and outside the classroom.

> **From Abby's Classroom**
>
> Starting in 2006 and for many years afterward, I consulted with a gifted and talented magnet school in Los Angeles whose students struggled with stress and anxiety related to yearly high-stakes testing, where students were consistently underperforming. Teachers led students through an array of stress-reduction exercises during testing season, but they were having no effect. That's when I was brought in.
>
> My first move was to ask students about their experiences with the stress-reduction exercises, which ranged from mindfulness-based practices to breathing techniques to journaling on their feelings about tests. Most students indicated that these exercises felt like a whole new subject they needed to learn and perfect, turning them from stress-reducing to stress-inducing. Students said the activities didn't feel connected to what they thought they should be doing, which was studying. In this case, administrators and teachers had been willing to commit the time necessary to help students find some sense of balance during testing, but students were still not having it. They rebelled against what they saw as a waste of precious time.
>
> It was clear to me that students were getting mixed messages. They were expected to achieve the highest possible test scores, but also asked to take time away from studying to do unfamiliar things. Students were so stressed about testing that they lost sleep as well as their appetites—not an auspicious combination.

My next move was to have a frank and earnest discussion with staff about their unsuccessful efforts. I posed a simple, pointed question: "How do you all feel about standardized testing?" Immediately, a litany of moans and eyerolls ensued. The educators said they felt pressured to ensure that their school produced high enough scores to maintain its reputation for excellence. This pressure turned to frustration when the methods they applied to reduce stress in students had the opposite effect.

I share this story to show that practices for stress modulation—what we refer to as *resources*—are not magic wands. Resourcing works when applied systemically and consistently. Time and again, I have been asked to contribute to projects and products that focus on reducing stress but fail to address its root causes. That's always a hard pass from me. I hope this book makes clearer the value of engaging students in a consistent and ongoing process of developing stress intelligence, including investigations into the *nature* of the origins of stress.

At the magnet school, I used stress-wise praxis to help the adults reflect on and reframe their views on testing. Most of them admitted to feeling discontent and unease about what felt like a major imposition on their ability to educate to their highest potential. As this awareness dawned, we turned our attention to the fact that the whole learning community was in distress, with no one reaching their potential in testing or otherwise. By identifying the pressure to maintain the school's reputation as the main source of distress, staff were able to reframe from centering test scores to centering well-being. Everyone agreed they would rather their school be known for having a compassionate learning community than for exerting high stress levels.

Leadership decided on several critical shifts in their approach. First, they would provide regular opportunities for their staff to develop their own stress IQs. Second, they would integrate body-mind-heart practices year-round rather than only during test time. Third, they would engage their whole community in this turn: At back-to-school nights and on their website, at parent-teacher conferences and through their PTA, they communicated that they needed to put wellness first. Not surprisingly, test scores went up.

When we approach resourcing from a resourced place within and with the intention to uplift well-being, our students are able to meet their full potential. Remember what really matters, and approach resourcing with a clear intention toward collective health and liberation. Yes, utilize body-mind-heart resources to support students during testing, but don't start or stop there. And by all means, put testing in its place as only one of many ways to assess learning.

The magnet school held up its promise to center well-being. Today, body-mind-heart practices are so integral to the school's culture that every meeting and event opens with a pause to connect to breath and become present. Students lead one another in regular resourcing. Now it is known as a school where people feel cared for as well as one that attains high test scores.

We are inspired by the many school communities that have taken the bold, stress-wise steps necessary to decenter high-stakes tests. The educators in these schools know that student achievement and well-being are inextricable from each other. Centering well-being gives learners the best chance at doing their best—but that well-being must be in service to the student, not the tests.

The resources that follow are meant to revitalize your learning environment with care, connection, and body-mind-heart integration.

# Learning Cycle 1
# Resourcing Ourselves:
# Practices to Further Understanding

**Objectives**
- Explore the concept of resourcing and how it can help to vitalize our ability to modulate stress and complete stress cycles.
- Practice pairing a known stressor with a potential resource through somatic and group exercises.

**Outcome**
- Students will gain the ability to modulate in response to feeling depleted or stressed.

**Keywords:** *resource, sustainable, vagus nerve*

## Phase 1.1: Engage
Matching Resources with Stressors

**Timeframe:** 10 minutes

**Class Discussion**

Ask students to name or list their responses to these questions:

- What is a resource?
- What natural resources do we utilize on a daily basis?
- What inner natural resources do we have?

**Activity**

One powerful way to tame stress is to acknowledge that it is present rather than ignoring or suppressing it. This allows us to break the cycle of reacting to stress by instead seeing it as a temporary state and conscientiously choosing to respond to it with a helpful resource.

For this activity, have students share or journal about resources that might orient them toward a solution or bring them relief in times of stress. Here are some sample responses:

- I am breathing.
- I feel the earth supporting me.
- I have dreams of better days.
- I have someone I can lean on for support.
- I love myself.

## Phase 1.2: Explore. Restoring Our Battery

**Timeframe:** 10 minutes

**Materials:** Figure 6.1

Show the device image in Figure 6.1 (see p. 120) and prompt students to think about this metaphor for being stress wise. The apps on this device represent the internal activity in the body, mind, and heart, and the battery life is our sense of vitality, which needs to be renewed as it becomes drained. If the device is not regularly recharged, it will cease to work well and may even shut down.

## Figure 6.1. A Metaphor for Draining or Recharging Our Vitality

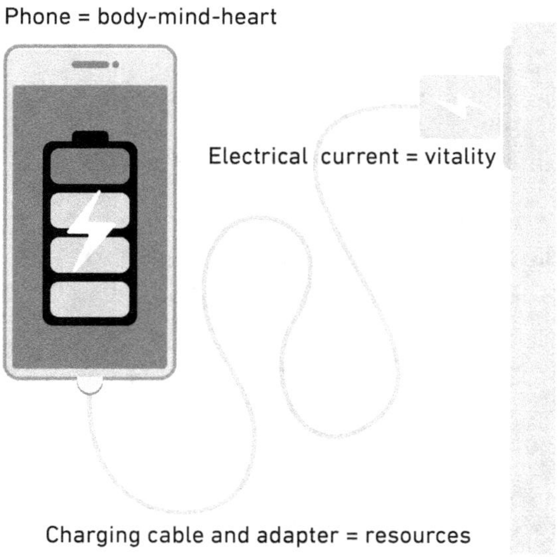

Phone = body-mind-heart

Electrical current = vitality

Charging cable and adapter = resources

Follow this script with your class:

> Imagine you are like the device in this image. You have a battery that lasts a certain amount of time and allows you to access all kinds of apps and connects with others near and far. A display shows you when your battery is running low, and you probably have an idea of how long it will take to get fully charged again.

Then, ask students the following questions:
- If you were a digital device right now, what would your battery life be?
- How do you know how much battery life you've got left (i.e., what are the physical or mental symptoms that signal to you it's time to recharge)?
- When was the last time you felt totally recharged? What did you plug into (i.e., what resources did you use) to recharge?
- What was happening the last time your battery died (i.e., when you felt totally depleted)?

If you notice students getting agitated as they reflect on these questions, prompt them to use their wisdom shift. Give them several minutes to contemplate their responses, then offer time for them to share their discoveries. Encourage everyone to listen intentionally to the speakers as they share how they navigate feeling drained and then experience being well resourced.

## Phase 1.3: Embody. Take a Break in Nature

**Timeframe:** 20 minutes

According to author Annie Murphy Paul (2021), we process sensory information more efficiently outdoors because the human brain evolved outdoors over thousands of years. Paul explains that being outdoors in natural settings prompts a more diffuse kind of attention, not in a scattered or disordered way, but in a rejuvenating way. When we witness the natural movements and contours of nature, a "soft fascination" emerges that contrasts with the harder-edged concentration we tend to use for learning. The wonderful result of this kind of soft fascination is that it actually *restores* our reserves of attention.

**Activity**

Plan some relaxed time outdoors with your students, perhaps at a nearby park or forest. The more natural the environment, the more effective it will be for resourcing your class. Long walks are ideal for restoring attention. Encourage students to use their five "wisdom channels"—sight, taste, smell, touch, and hearing—to fully and mindfully experience being outdoors.

## Phase 1.4: Expand. A Major Internal Resource

**Timeframe:** 10–15 minutes

**Materials:** Figures 6.2 and 6.3

Show students Figures 6.2 and 6.3 (see p. 122) and read or paraphrase the following script:

> The vagus nerve is part of our hardware of well-being. It functions within the parasympathetic nervous system to help us remain in and return to our natural, vital state of being. Through regulated breathing patterns and certain movements, we can intentionally recruit the inherent power of our vagus nerve, an ally that helps us get through stress and thrive (Rosenberg, 2017).

**Figure 6.2. The Vagus Nerve**

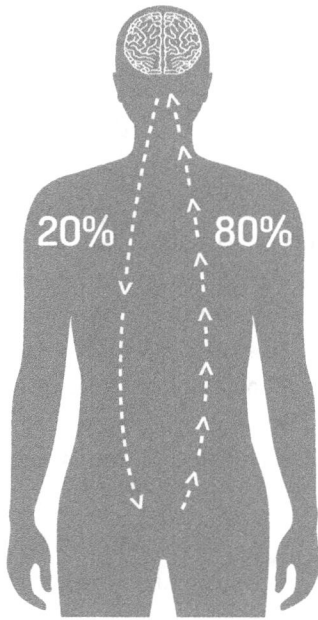

Eighty percent of the vagus nerve fibers send messages from the body to the brain, whereas only 20 percent send messages from the brain to the body.

**Figure 6.3. The Vagus Nerve's Connections to the Rest of the Body**

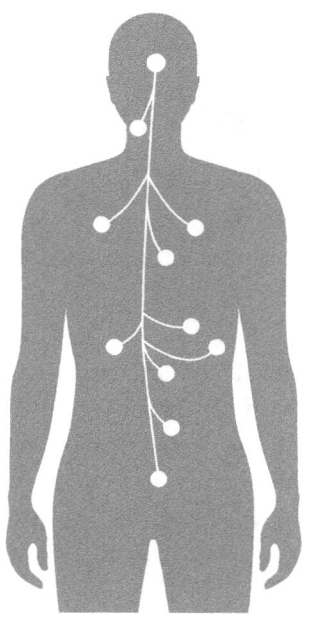

Continue with the following script:

> The vagus nerve is nicknamed "the wandering nerve" because it travels from the brain to many parts of the body, including the stomach, liver, spleen, gallbladder, pancreas, small intestine, bladder, kidneys, and parts of the colon. Among other things, it helps to regulate heart rate and allows us to feel socially engaged, safe, and social. Its unique anatomical position throughout the body makes it a sort of surveillance system, always monitoring for potential threats and alerting the amygdala when our internal alarm needs to be sounded. The vagus nerve helps us to sense if there is anything to be stressed about and, if not, allows relaxation to ensue.

Now ask students, "How might conscious breathing practices help us engage the vagus nerve to our benefit?" (Hint: look for where the respiratory diaphragm and vagus nerve intersect.) Give students time to research their answer.

## Phase 1.5: Express. Resourcing Yourself Check-In

**Timeframe:** 10–20 minutes

Ask students to consider where they are on the stress–vitality spectrum and journal about it. Remind them that detecting when your battery is running very low and regularly recharging helps to keep our devices working well for a long time. Rather than plugging in and resourcing for more energy only when we feel completely depleted, we can sustain our energy levels with regular charging.

Next, ask students the following questions:

- What foods and drinks, activities, people, circumstances, or other things drain your battery?
- What are the signals your body, mind, and emotions display to let you know you need to recharge soon?
- When your mind is not working at 100 percent power, how do you know?
- When your heart needs to recharge, how do you know?
- From a stress-wise point of view, what do you think is the "electricity" that charges and animates us when we are drained?

Have students journal about at least four things they "plugged into" this week to get their energy back. These could include activities, objects, foods, people, or something else that helps them to feel revitalized and fully powered up. Here are some sample student responses:

- My mom
- Skateboarding
- Music
- Working out
- Sleeping
- Friends
- The ocean

# Learning Cycle 2
# Discharge Stress and Recharge Vitality

**Objective**
- Learn how perception influences our experience of stress.

**Outcome**
- Students learn how to use resourcing when experiencing mental and physical fatigue.

**Keywords:** *perception, overstimulation*

## Phase 2.1: Engage. Thoughts Are Influencers

**Timeframe:** 10 minutes

Students may sit or stand for the following short exploration. Follow this script with your class:

> Imagine you are waiting at a bus stop to visit a good friend. Sit or stand as you normally would while waiting.
> 
> The bus is taking longer than expected. You are concerned that you will miss out on time to hang out with your friend. Notice how you feel in your body.

The bus is now approaching. Notice how you feel as you prepare to board the bus. What thoughts do you have at this moment?

Instead of stopping, the bus passes you by.

Pause and notice what you feel in your body. What thoughts arise?

Twenty-five minutes pass, and there is no bus in sight. How do you feel? Frustrated? Disappointed? Stressed out? Anxious? Angry? [Call on students to describe how they feel.]

Just as you are losing hope that you will get to see your friend, a car pulls up to the bus stop. You realize it is your friend and their caregiver coming to pick you up! Notice any changes in how your body feels as you imagine greeting your friend. How do you feel? Relieved? Safe? Happy? [Call on students to describe how they feel.]

Look at all these different emotions and feelings we experienced in the past few minutes. What actually changed? We are still here in the same room. There are no buses or cars. The only things that changed were our thoughts. On purpose, we changed what we were imagining. In doing so, our bodies responded with different sensations. This is an example of how perceived stress works.

## Phase 2.2: Explore. Draining the Stress Sink

**Timeframe:** 15–20 minutes

**Materials:** Figure 6.4

Show students the image in Figure 6.4 (see p. 126). Then, follow this script with your class:

Imagine that the sink is your body. The hot and cold knobs on the sink represent the perceived and real stressors that turn on your stress response, allowing the symptoms of stress to flow into the sink. If the sink is what "collects" our stress symptoms like sweating, faster heart rate, tunnel vision, and quick thinking, what does the drain represent? [Give students time to reflect and respond.]

## Figure 6.4. Stress Sink

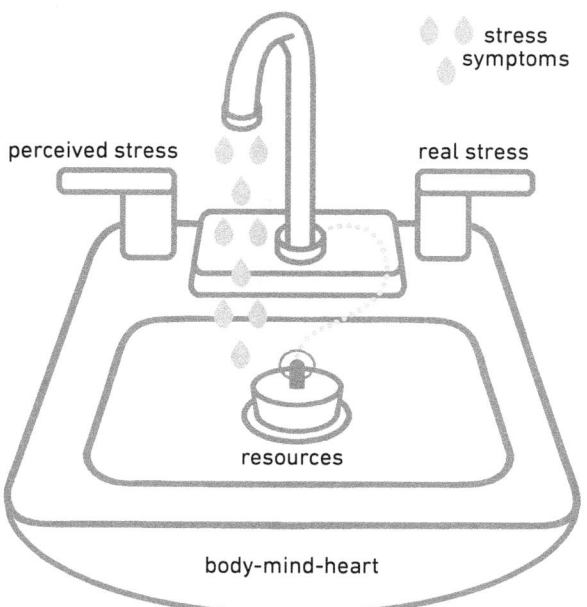

What allows us to "drain" our stress and find relief? [If necessary, note that this kind of "draining" is different from the draining of a battery as discussed in Phase 1.2.]

Resourcing is the drain of the stress sink. Resourcing helps us to complete the stress cycle after it begins from either of its two sources and allows us to regulate back to homeostasis, where integration and adaptation take shape. Accessing our resources makes the difference between a sink that overflows and a sink that empties—that is, between chronic stress that lacks resolution and acute stress that we get through with a sense of relief.

### Small-Group Activity

Have students share and discuss the following:

- Two things that cause their stress sink to overflow
- Two things that act like a drain and help them to experience relief from stress

If students are inspired by one of their classmates' ways to drain stress, they should make a note of it in their journal and share their gratitude for the inspiration with the classmate. When students are done sharing, conclude by saying the following:

> Reframing our stress with tools we can use to get through it is inspiring and promotes individual and collective well-being. Instead of only complaining about what stresses you out, how does it feel to share about what helps you move through and coexist with stress?

## Phase 2.3: Embody. Eye and Mind Reset Practice

**Timeframe:** 10 minutes

Invite students to sit, lean, or stand in a way that allows them to feel resourced and centered. Once they're settled, follow this script:

> Our physical eyes are so powerful. They allow us to see into the world around us, find what and whom we are looking for, access resources, detect threats, and solve problems. Just like animals in the wild, when we concentrate on a task, our eyes focus and our pupils narrow. This can happen even when we're scrolling on our phones. When our eyes are concentrating, our stress response activates because our nervous system doesn't know if we're stalking our prey, tracking a predator from a clever hiding place, or browsing social media on a small screen.
> 
>   Let's practice resting our eyes, disconnecting from a narrow focus linked with stress and reconnecting to a sense of ease and big-picture thinking. If you're wearing glasses, please set them down and tune in through your sense of hearing. Gently close your eyes or lower your gaze and begin to rub your hands together, building up some heat between them. Hear the sound your hands make as they rub together. Feel the texture of your palms and notice the heat building between them. Once your hands feel

> warm, cup them over your eyes, blocking out all the ambient light in the room. [Pause, noticing if any students take a spontaneous deep breath, sigh, or yawn.]
>
> Without pressing too hard, allow the skin of your palms to make as much contact with your face as you can. Sense your hands pressed along the round bone of your eye socket, your eyebrows, cheekbone, and the edge of your nose. [Pause.]
>
> As your hands shield your eyes from the light, imagine them also shielding your eyes and mind from any incoming information. [Pause.] With less to do now, imagine how it might feel for the back of your eyes to widen in their sockets, releasing any tunnel vision from concentrating too hard. [Pause.] Stay like this if it feels nourishing, or slowly move your eyes from side to side like slow-motion windshield wipers, clearing away mental fog and distraction. [Pause.]
>
> Stay like this for a few more moments, allowing your eyes to rest. When you feel ready to move on, release your hands and blink a few times to reopen your eyes. Can you keep a softer quality to your gaze with your eyes open?

Invite students to share their experiences aloud or in their journals. Draw the connection between resting our eyes and draining the stress sink to feel less overwhelmed.

## Phase 2.4: Expand. Power of Perception

**Timeframe:** 15 minutes

Follow this script with your class:

> We know that experiencing a stressor creates a cycle of stress. Some stressors come from the outside and are tangible—getting chased by a tiger, for example, or seeing the bus leave right before we get to the stop. Other stressors come from our perceptions or imagination.
>
> Imagine that you are very scared of snakes. You are camping at night with friends and need to get more kindling for the fire.

Leaving your flashlight behind, you walk into the woods and see something in the grass that looks like a snake. You scream and yell for your friends, who come running with a flashlight to your rescue. They shine the light on the snake only to discover that it is a discarded piece of rope from previous campers.

In this scenario, there is no real threat to your safety, only a perceived threat. Does your body still experience a stress response? The great news is that we can control perceived stress.

What are some examples of perceived stress in your life—stressors that seem to be very threatening and cause you to feel scared or nervous but don't actually pose a real or tangible threat to you? Name some emotional or psychological stressors that create a feeling of stress in your physical body. [Hold space for students to convey their thoughts.]

How can you tell if you are reacting to a perceived stressor? What can you do to deactivate stress when you realize you are reacting to something that is not threatening you in the moment? [Again, hold space for students to respond.]

Close this activity with two or three minutes of a breathing practice or other activity that your class has found helpful for regulating stress.

## Phase 2.5: Express
### DIY or Resource Inventory Show-and-Tell

**Timeframe:** 20 minutes

Think about the most enlivening way for your class to integrate the information from this learning cycle. What form of expression would best help you to assess student understanding? Consider designing an activity or formulating a journal prompt to cap this learning cycle.

You may also invite students to create and share their "resource inventory"—a list of people, places, activities, and things that allow them to navigate away from unhealthy zones of stress and return to a "healthy stress zone." Prompt students to share ways they drain emotional stress, physical stress, mental stress, and social stress. They can also show or teach movement practices to their classmates that help them drain their stress. These could be techniques they have learned through the stress-wise framework or from other areas of their life.

Remind students that wisdom comes from within, and that it is gained over time with life experience. Ask them where they feel they could be wiser when it comes to stress. Acknowledge how far everyone has come already and that participating in practices and conversations like the ones in the stress-wise framework strengthens connection to the voice of wisdom.

# Learning Cycle 3
# Your Breath Is a Free Resource

**Objective**
- Delve into breath as a central resource for modulation.

**Outcome**
- Students will gain awareness of the power of breathing.

**Keywords:** *breath, coregulation*

## Phase 3.1: Engage. Necessary Resources

**Timeframe:** 5 minutes

**Class Discussion**

Share these prompts with students:

- What is essential to life?
- Name the things we cannot live without.

Point out that of all life's essentials, breathing is the one thing we cannot live without for longer than a few minutes. It is essential from the moment we are born until the moment we die. (Consider pairing Phases 3.1 and 3.2.)

## Phase 3.2: Explore. Breathing with Partners

**Timeframe:** 10 minutes

**Dyad Activity**

This activity can be a powerful experience of coregulation, but it requires a degree of vulnerability. In advance, ask students who you feel will be inclined to participate readily to normalize the experience by demonstrating the activity. Consider playing music to hold a stronger container for the activity.

Students sit back-to-back on the floor with a classmate. Give them time to settle. If they resist, remind them that they are simply two human beings sitting down. Instruct them to sit in such a way that both students feel supported when they lean back on each other. Ideally, students will sit upright so there is as much contact between them as possible, from the sacrum to the cranium.

Once students are settled in their postures, ask them to relax their eyes and begin to deepen their breathing. Ask them to notice where they can feel their partner's breath moving in their own back. Over time, students can synchronize their breathing and even direct their breaths to the same parts of their back (upper, middle, lower). Allow three to five minutes for students to explore their breathing with a classmate.

To conclude, invite students to share one word to describe the experience. At the magnet school where Abby worked, this practice helped to ease stress and build trust, and students shared such words as *connected, relaxed, mindful, supported,* and *calming.* Encourage your students to try this activity with a family member or a friend who helps them feel recharged.

## Phase 3.3: Embody. 3D Breath Experience

**Timeframe:** 20 minutes

Instruct students to sit in a posture that allows them to feel tall and alert. Then, share the following script:

> Either bring your awareness to the circumference of your lower ribs or place your hands around them to get a better idea of this part of your body. Our respiratory diaphragm is considered the

"muscle of breathing" because it helps to pull air into our lungs and push air out of them, changing the shape and volume of our chest cavity. It lives beneath the lungs across the bottom of the rib cage and above the stomach and is shaped like an oval or the top of an umbrella. Can you sense your diaphragm or imagine what it might look like?

Bring awareness to the front section of your lower ribs. You're welcome to place a hand across them to focus your attention. Take a slow, deep inhale, sensing your ribs expanding forward toward your shirt. Take three more breath cycles, exploring how your front ribs and diaphragm move. [Pause.]

Now bring attention to your side lower ribs. Feel free to bring your hands to them. Take three to four deep, slow inhales and try to sense your ribs widening outward as you breathe. [Pause.]

Touch your back ribs or lean back into your chair. Take three or four more slow, mindful breaths, feeling how your back ribs expand backward with each inhale. Take a few more breaths on your own. Sense your body in 3D.

As students are breathing, read the following quote from *Breath: The New Science of a Lost Art* (2021) by James Nestor:

> In a single breath, more molecules of air will pass through your nose than all the grains of sand on all the world's beaches—trillions and trillions of them. These little bits of air come from a few feet or several yards away. As they make their way toward you, they'll twist and spool like the stars in a van Gogh sky, and they'll keep twisting and spooling and scrolling as they pass into you, traveling at a clip of about five miles per hour. (p. 44)

Then, continue with this script:

Continue to breathe calmly. Sense or visualize the air molecules traveling toward and through your body, revitalizing you the way a charger reenergizes a digital device. [Pause.]

Begin to notice where your feet are. Remember where you're sitting in the room. When you feel ready, blink your eyes open.

At this point, invite students to share anything they felt or noticed during this exercise.

## Phase 3.4: Expand
### Breathing Patterns to Modulate Stress

**Timeframe:** 5–10 minutes

Breathing is a universal resource that has a profound effect on the human body. Just like food, breathing connects us with the world outside the body. Intentional breathing can help reduce stress, prevent insomnia, regulate emotions, and improve attention. On a physical level, it can also increase immunity and reduce our risk of disorders like high blood pressure, heart disease, lung disease, and diabetes (André, 2019).

The power of breathing lies in its ability to help us regulate our central nervous system. Even though breathing is an involuntary behavior, when we bring awareness to the process, we can use the breath as a resource to increase our health and reduce stress (Bordoni et al., 2018).

**5-2-6 Breathing Pattern Exercise**

Ask students to follow these steps:

1. Inhale deeply through the nose for a count of five.
2. Hold your breath for a count of two.
3. Exhale completely through the mouth for a count longer than five.

According to Harvard professor Herbert Benson (1976), controlled breathing of this sort triggers our parasympathetic nervous system to counteract our sympathetic nervous system, calming us down.

Ask students, "What are some times in your life when you paused and took a deep breath to help you slow down and become more present?"

**Dig Deeper**

Follow this script with your class:

> Did you know that throughout the day we switch between breathing predominantly through one nostril more than the other? Can you place your hand under your nostrils and tell which nostril is more active?

Breathing predominantly through the right nostril is like pressing the gas pedal—body temperature, stress hormones, circulation, and blood pressure all increase. The sympathetic nervous system is activated to create a sense of alertness to protect us from danger. By contrast, breathing predominantly through the left nostril is like hitting the brakes—parasympathetic activation lowers our blood pressure, cools our body, and can reduce anxiety. For thousands of years, yoga practices have taught us to intentionally alternate the nostrils we breathe through and to bring attention to left-nostril breathing when we are in a state of stress (Nestor, 2021).

## Phase 3.5: Express. What Takes Our Breath Away

**Timeframe:** 10 minutes

In this learning cycle, we've started to explore the incredible influence breathing has on how well we feel and think. Breathing is three-dimensional, and each breath happens in a four-part cycle: inhale, pause after the inhale; exhale, pause after the exhale. So far in this chapter, we have explored some breathing patterns that play with the rhythm or length of this cycle. Because intentional breathing can change how we think and feel, it is a resource we can use to help us feel more alert or relaxed when necessary.

We'll end this LC by building a bridge between intentional breathing and moments in real life that influence our breathing.

**Journaling Prompts**

Ask students to respond to these prompts in their journal:

1. What takes your breath away? Write about or draw something that makes you feel breathless. This could be something emotional in nature, like something so incredibly beautiful that you feel swept away in its beauty, or something that strikes you as so shocking that the sight or thought of it stops your breath momentarily.
2. What gives your breath a boost? Write or draw about an activity or experience that either helps you breathe better or more freely or requires you to breathe more deeply.

# Learning Cycle 4
# Rest Is Replenishing

**Objectives**
- Reveal the importance of repose for vitality.
- Examine the resourceful nature of sleep.

**Outcome**
- Students will apply resourcing to support mental and physical fatigue.

**Keywords:** *sleep, hygiene, repose*

## Phase 4.1: Engage. Repose Versus Sleep

**Timeframe:** 10–15 minutes

**Class Discussion**

Hold a whole-class discussion around these prompts:

- What is the difference between rest and sleep?
- How do you know when you are resting, and how do you know when you are sleeping?
- What is repose?
- We know why sleep is important. How does resting add to our well-being, and where can you personally see adding in more deliberate time in your week to rest?

Encourage students to consider how mindfulness and awareness contribute to our experiences of repose and sleep, reminding them that one is done while conscious and the other while unconscious. Conscious rest, or intentionally resting without sleeping, is a special way of resourcing ourselves and a way to recharge ourselves mentally, emotionally, and physically.

## Phase 4.2: Explore. Playlist for Repose

**Timeframe:** 15 minutes

**Small-Group Activity**

Students connect in their small groups to discuss and list "symptoms of relaxation": what relaxation feels like in their bodies, minds, and hearts. Prompt each group to select a song or two to add to a class playlist of relaxing music. (You can repurpose this playlist at your discretion and pair it with any of the activities in this book.)

## Phase 4.3: Embody. Conscious Rest Meditation

**Timeframe:** 20 minutes

**Materials:** blankets, large towels, or mats; video at www.youtube.com/ @StressWisePractices-wo3kv

For this deeply restorative practice, students will be lying down. Recruit students to assist with any special arrangements needed to make space in the room and to reassemble after the practice. Some students may feel most comfortable with something covering their body, like a jacket or something similar. Encourage students to take a few minutes to make themselves feel safe and comfortable. If you notice any restlessness, suggest that students place one hand over their chest and the other over their abdomen. Once everyone has settled, follow the link to play the audio practice or read aloud the following script.

> In this meditation, we are practicing deep relaxation without sleeping. I invite you to close your eyes and let your eye muscles start to rest. Follow the sound of my voice during this practice, and if your mind wanders away, that is OK; just bring your attention back to the sound of my voice. Begin to breathe in and out through your nose gently. Imagine that your belly is a balloon and as you inhale, feel your belly inflate, stretching up and out a little bit. As you exhale, feel your belly deflate softly. Continue to breathe like this.
>
> We're going to practice relaxing all the muscles in our body by first tensing them up and then relaxing them. Tighten both of your hands into fists, as much as you can, squeeze-*squeeze,* and now release them. Tighten your arms, make them really tense, now let them go. Scrunch up your toes, squeeze them tightly, and let them relax completely. Tighten your leg muscles, make your muscles feel hard and tense, and now let your legs completely relax. Slide

your shoulders up toward your ears, tighten everything up, and now let them slide down and relax toward the floor. Scrunch up your face really tight. Tighten your nose, forehead, eyes, cheeks, like you ate something really sour, and now smooth and relax your whole face. Smooth and soften every muscle, everywhere. Let all that tension go.

Now we'll practice counting our breath. Breathe in while mentally saying the number 27, and as you breathe out, say to yourself the number 27. The next inhale is 26, and the next exhale, say to yourself 26. Keep counting backward all the way down to 1. [Pause.] If you lose count, begin again at 27.

There's no need to rush. Dismiss any distracting thoughts and counting, counting down in your mind. Don't get frustrated if you miss a number. Be kind to your mind if it wants to wander or fall asleep. It doesn't matter if you get to 1; just practice counting your breath.

Now let the counting go. Relax your mind all the way.

We're going to be moving the mind around different parts of your relaxed body, like taking a tour of your body with your mind. When your mind moves to each part, it's as if it shines a warm golden light onto it. Giving it vitality and peace. There's no need to move that part of your body—just move your imagination to that part of your body. Beginning now with your left-hand thumb, index finger, third finger, ring finger, pinkie, palm, wrist, forearm, elbow, shoulder, all radiant with golden light. Move to the right-hand thumb, index finger, third finger, ring finger, pinkie, palm, wrist, forearm, elbow, shoulder, the whole right arm filled with radiant golden light. Move down to the left big toe, second toe, third toe, fourth toe, pinkie toe, foot, ankle, knee, thigh, left hip, and now to your right big toe, second toe, third toe, fourth toe, pinkie toe . . . foot, ankle, knee, thigh, right hip . . . imagine both legs bright with warm golden light. Move that warm light to your lower back, your upper back, your neck, head, top of your head, left ear, right ear, left eyebrow, right eyebrow, left eye, right eye, tip of your nose, left cheek, right cheek, upper lip, lower lip, jaw, your tongue, throat, chest, your heart, filled with warm radiant light, your belly ... your whole body gently glowing with the light of vitality and peace. Sense this in your whole body. Every part.

Now we'll share that light from our wise self with the people in this world whom we love and who help us feel safe and loved ... bring them to your mind now, sharing this peaceful light with them. Your best friends, your parents, your teachers, pets, and siblings ... your role models ... your classmates ... and now we'll send some of that light to other people in the world who need some peace and warmth in their lives and send some from your heart to them ... and imagine the world sending that energy right back to you as you send it out.

Now breathe into your belly, expanding like a balloon. Feel your belly rise, and fall. You are wonderful. You are safe. You are important and the world needs your light and your talent. Take a few big breaths on your own, letting your mind and body feel more awake. Then slowly roll over to one side for a moment. You can yawn or sigh and let go of this conscious rest practice. Bring yourself upright to sit.

---

Deep rest became a favorite at the magnet school where Abby worked. The PTA eventually purchased mats, blankets, and eye pillows to enhance the experience. Once a month, the school yoga teacher would set up the auditorium as a cozy zone for rest and classes would rotate through for 30-minute sessions. The whole school felt more balanced for days to come. You may notice that your students are sleepy or quite energized after this practice. Give them a few minutes to regroup before moving into the next lesson on the agenda, including drinking some water, journaling their experience, or sharing where they are on the stress–vitality spectrum now that they've had some time to rest.

**Alternative:** Repeat Eye and Mind Reset Practice from Phase 2.3 (p. 127).

## Phase 4.4: Expand. Science of Sleep

**Timeframe:** 10 minutes

Read aloud or paraphrase the following script, or ask a student to read it aloud.

Sleep is integral to all processes in the human body, including metabolism, cognition, memory, muscle tone development, and the proper functioning of all our organs. During sleep, our bodies are able to rest and recover from stress, making us more resilient to our daily troubles and allowing our stress to drain (Walker, 2017).

Restful sleep is generally seven to nine hours long and enables us to wake up easily and with a sense of vitality (Suni & Truong, 2022). Humans tend to follow a circadian rhythm: we go to bed at a reasonable hour once the sun sets, and we wake just before sunrise to make the most of sunlight's helpful influence. Circadian rhythm enhances our mood and boosts our immunity; every single organ in our body has circadian genes that correspond to our bodily clock (Panda, 2020). When we are in a routine sleep/wake cycle and surrounded by natural light, each organ in our body functions at a higher capacity.

Staying up into the early hours of the morning or sleeping into the afternoon can be detrimental to our health and mood, and most adolescents have unbalanced sleeping patterns. According to one recent study, 57.8 percent of middle schoolers and 72 percent of high schoolers get less than the recommended amount of sleep for their age (Centers for Disease Control and Prevention, 2019). One of the biggest challenges to adequate sleep is the use of electronics in the evening (Singh & Suni, 2022). Cell phones, tablets, and laptops all put out a blue light that halts the body's production of melatonin, the hormone that helps us feel sleepy. For this reason, it is important for sleep hygiene to disconnect from our electronics one to two hours before bed.

Now share the following tips for getting the most out of sleep:

- Help reset your day-night clock by going outside to view early-morning light after waking.
- Give your body a chance to experience rest during the day with a midday break of deep breathing or a visualization.
- Dim the lights one to two hours before bed to signal sleep to your brain by mimicking dusk and sunset indoors.

## Phase 4.5: Express. Repose and Sleep Check-In

**Timeframe:** 10 minutes

**Journaling Prompts**

Ask students to respond to these prompts in their journal:

- What challenges can get in the way of sleeping enough?
- What foods or drinks promote sleep? Which ones promote wakefulness?
- How do you know you feel rested?
- How does being tired affect your mood and your ability to learn?
- What boundaries can you set to improve your sleep? (Hint: think about how factors like using devices or exercise might impact your ability to fall asleep.)

# Learning Cycle 5
# Compassion: A Heartful Resource

**Objectives**
- Develop language around compassion, boundaries, and self-acceptance.
- Practice self-compassion.

**Outcomes**
- Students will be able to set and respect compassionate boundaries for personal and collective stress modulation.
- A curious, compassionate classroom culture

**Keywords:** *compassion, self-compassion, soothing, boundaries*

## Phase 5.1: Engage
### Exploring Compassion and Boundaries

**Timeframe:** 10–20 minutes

**Compassion Inquiry**

Use any or all of the following open-ended inquiries to prompt discussion. Invite students to answer with any thoughts that arise. Let them know you are not looking for a "right" answer but, rather, are interested in their exploration on the topic:

- What is compassion?
- Where does compassion come from?
- Who do you know who is compassionate among your family, friends, or community?
- What are boundaries? Can you give an example of a compassionate boundary?

While guiding the discussion, acknowledge and point out connections between students' responses. Use the following prompts to deepen the dialogue:

- Why is compassion important?
- How can we apply compassion when we notice stress building in our systems?
- How can compassion support us in our response to stressful situations?
- What boundaries can we set in our classroom to help make our collective space feel more welcoming and easier to learn in?
- What boundaries can we set with ourselves to decrease stress and pressure when we feel it building?

The last two questions here were particularly helpful for students at the magnet school where Abby worked. They discovered together that when fellow students were encouraging and kind to one another during testing, the emotional tone in the classroom was more supportive of their process. One of the classes adopted a practice of pausing to take a few deep breaths in and out before taking a test, then the teacher would count to three before the class chanted in unison, "We got this!" This simple pause and collective refrain of support set students up with courage and a feeling of connection, rather than entering the test with a feeling of dread.

Through discussions on personal boundaries, students at the magnet school discovered a variety of ways to resource themselves during the elevated stress of testing. Prioritizing sleep rather than obsessively studying into the early morning hours equipped students with more energy to do their best. Students also often pointed to the need to set strong boundaries with social media and internet browsing when they were trying to focus. As one student wisely shared, "It could just be three minutes checking out the new Supreme drop, but then that keeps popping up in my head all day. I don't need to be thinking about that when I'm trying to remember a thousand other facts, so I save that stuff for after the test is done and I did my best, like a reward."

## Phase 5.2: Explore
### Common Humanity Is Part of Compassion

**Timeframe:** 10–20 minutes

Say to students, "Compassion is a seed planted in every one of us from an early age. As our compassion grows, the seed develops roots and eventually flowers. In this activity, we will create a garden of compassion by sharing our common humanity."

Next, have students stand in a circle to create a "garden bed" for the garden of compassion that will be planted while a volunteer reads out the following prompts:

Step into the circle if you have ever . . .

- Reached out to a friend who was having a hard time.
- Missed a friend who moved away.
- Shared your lunch with someone who forgot theirs.
- Helped someone with homework.
- Given someone a gift that you really wanted for yourself.
- Had to set a boundary with someone you love.
- Offered someone the benefit of the doubt.
- Picked up litter.

For every statement students agree with, they step into the center of the circle, take a look around the circle, then step back out before the next statement. Ask students to continue coming up with phrases. End the activity by having volunteers share how it felt to see their common humanity demonstrated.

## Phase 5.3: Embody. Self-Compassionate Touch

**Timeframe:** 5–10 minutes

One of the ways our nervous system can receive signals of safety is through self-soothing touch. Think of healing touch as nourishment for the nervous system: By placing one or both hands on different parts of the body, we can offer the nervous system a way to pump the brakes and rest.

For this activity, invite students to find a comfortable seat, then follow this script:

> Begin by placing one hand over the center of your chest. Notice how this feels in your body. If this is comforting, take a few breaths here. If not, you can release your hand to where it feels most comfortable.
>
> Place both hands on your collarbones with a very soft touch. If you find this comforting, take a few deep breaths here. If not, return your hands to a comfortable position.
>
> Place both hands on your cheeks with a very gentle, light touch. If you find this comforting, take a few deep breaths here. If not, return your hands to a comfortable position.

Invite students to find a variation that is soothing for them. Encourage them to trust the "symptoms of relaxation" their body signals to them as a way of knowing which variation suits them best. Options may include a hand on the belly and a hand on the heart, both hands over the ears, or both hands on the center of the chest.

Once their hands are in their comforting place, invite students to imagine receiving a sense of comfort with every inhale they take. Ask, "What does comfort feel like? How does it change your body?"

When you are done, have students discuss the exercise: "How was this practice for you? What can you learn from the sensations in your body?"

## Phase 5.4: Expand. Two Styles of Self-Compassion

**Timeframe:** 5 minutes

Read aloud or paraphrase the following script, or ask a student to read it aloud.

> Compassion literally means to feel another's pain in your heart. Emotion researchers (Strauss et al., 2016) define compassion as the feeling that arises when you are confronted with another's

suffering and feel motivated to relieve that suffering. Much as our sympathetic nervous system warns us to escape or avoid a threat, compassion prompts us to help relieve the suffering of others.

When we turn this compassion toward ourselves, we develop self-compassion, which means extending patience, kindness, and understanding to ourselves as we would to others, especially when we are having a difficult time. Self-compassion begins when we meet ourselves with kindness rather than self-judgment (Bluth, 2017). We learn to accept that we are not perfect and embrace this reality with kindness. In this process of acceptance, we recognize that everyone struggles, everyone has a hard time, and no one is perfect. Practicing kindness and acceptance like this develops our skills of compassion and can help us to relieve stress around perfectionism.

Developing self-compassion requires patience and mindful awareness. When we get caught in a spiral of thoughts that rev our metaphorical stress engine, self-compassion can help bring us back to a more neutral place of acceptance that can alleviate suffering.

This tender form of self-compassion is how we learn to become kindhearted in the face of suffering. However, sometimes we need a fiercer form of self-compassion that helps us to make changes, thrive, and develop an authentic self (Neff, 2022). Sometimes self-compassion can look like saying no by setting a boundary around our time, the foods we eat, or the technology we use to avoid feeling drained or burned out.

How can you know which type of self-compassion is appropriate in a given situation? What signals do your body, mind, and heart give you when you need to be tender and when you need to be fierce?

## Phase 5.5: Express. Summon Your Self-Compassion

**Timeframe:** 20 minutes

Follow these steps with your class, having them record their responses in their journals:

1. Ask students to write down what compassion means to them.
2. Ask students to write a short letter to a friend who is having a hard time. What would they say to their friend? How might they console them?
3. Ask students if they would use the same kind of language with themselves. It is common to be harder on ourselves than on others. Learning how to speak to ourselves with compassion is a practice that will grow over time as we bring increasing awareness to our tendencies.
4. Ask students to practice writing to themselves in a kind voice. If they are having trouble, it can help to think of a friend, mentor, or family member who has a compassionate voice. What would they say during a hard time? Here are some sentence stems to suggest:
    - I am proud of you for ...
    - You are doing great at ...
    - Your strengths are ...
    - This will get easier as ...
    - For me, fierce compassion looks like ...
    - For me, tender compassion looks like ...

# Learning Cycle 6
# From Animal Kingdom to Microbiome

**Objectives**
- Practice ways to discharge a stress response through physicality.
- Explore how food and nature are resources for vitality.

**Outcomes**
- Students will develop an awareness of specific movement practices and foods that promote vitality and decrease stress.
- Students will be inspired to find resources in daily activities.

**Keyword:** *enteric nervous system*

# Phase 6.1: Engage
## Discharge Stress: Animal Breath Edition

**Timeframe:** 20 minutes

**Materials (optional):** talking piece (preferably a natural object)

If possible, go outdoors for this phase. Form a circle and consider passing a talking piece around so each student has an opportunity to respond. Encourage students to listen to each other mindfully, without judgment, and in a kind and curious manner.

Share with students that a growing body of research shows that nature is one of the most powerful resources for effectively recovering from stress because it boosts our immunity, mood, and even metabolism. Pose the following creative prompts:

- If you could be an animal for a day, which one would you choose and why? (e.g., a falcon so I could fly ultra-fast; a sloth so I could rest all day).
- Name a part of nature that represents how you feel in your life right now and why (e.g., I feel like a river flowing; I feel like a tree because I am branching out).

Share with students that breathing is integral to all nature. Ask them how they think animals might change their breath to release stress, then share the following breathing practices influenced by the natural world:

- **Bee breath:** Breathe in deeply. Breathe out with your mouth closed, and huuuuuummm like a bee. How long can you make your humming exhale here?
- **Lion breath:** Breathe in through the nose. Open your mouth wide, and as you exhale, *roaaaaaarrr* out your breath. Try again and see if you can make the exhale longer and louder.

Ask, "Can you think of any other animals that might have a special breath? What about an elephant or a crocodile?"

Students at the magnet school where Abby worked always engaged fully in determining and sharing their chosen animal for a day and the parts of nature they felt connected to. They loved learning more about one another in this activity than they did in typical academic experiences. The sense of connection and belonging students feel when they are able to reveal something special about themselves is a powerful resource for stress reduction.

## Phase 6.2: Explore
### Discharge Stress: Animal Movement Edition

**Timeframe:** 15 minutes

Energy regulation through exercise, meditation, and contemplative practices like mindfulness and journaling is an essential pillar of health and vitality. To complete a cycle of stress, we usually need a physical discharge, which can be found through somatic practices like yoga, dancing, running, and other forms of movement. Because stress is a physiological response, discharging stress through movement is one of the most practical tools for developing a stress-wise classroom. Without it, stress builds up in the system, leading to increased anxiety, depression, and frustration as well as increased levels of inflammation, which can lead to disease. Movement can enhance our playful nature, leading to greater healing and joy in our lives. Animals often shake, run, or move in creative ways after they experience a stressor, and we can learn from this wisdom by inviting a regular movement practice to help regulate energy.

**Learning from Animals**

Follow these steps with your class:

1. Invite students to stand in a large circle. Say, "Let's begin an exploration of how stress cycles can live in our bodies. Animals are wonderful examples in the natural world of how our bodies can see and perceive chronic stress. Let's play with this idea a little!"
2. Invite students to move like a butterfly, using light, airy, flowing movements. Spend 30–60 seconds exploring this movement.
3. Say, "Now imagine that the butterfly had too much sugar and was feeling very hyper. How would the butterfly move? Shaky, fast, frenetic movements are what we feel when we have been stretched past our capacity. When our bodies act in this way, it is clear that we need to find time for grounding."

4. Invite students to move like a tiger: regal, confident, strong, and purposeful. Say, "What happens when the tiger feels threatened? How does the tiger move in this state? It becomes angry, hot, watchful, and impatient. This is just how we feel when we are pushed beyond our limit and are experiencing a fight response. Slowing down, getting lots of sleep, and hydrating are very important for cooling down!"
5. Say, "How would you imagine a baby elephant would stand? How would it move when it plays in the water? It would probably use gentle, slow, and thoughtful movements. How does a baby elephant move when it feels safe and loved?"
6. Say, "Suddenly the baby elephant looks up and notices that its mother is missing! How does the baby elephant respond? We usually feel a frozen panic in response to this kind of shock or stressor. To come back to our bodies, we need to learn how to orient to find safety. We can do so by looking around and asking for help from the people around us."
7. Ask, "Which animal most resonated with you? How can you learn from the animals to better respond to stress?"

After we offered this activity for student leaders in grades 7–12 at a summit, one student remarked that their main takeaway was that "your mental health helps determine what type of leader you are." Students emphasized their need to better regulate sleep, food choices, and physical exercise now that they had learned about their effects on stress. Another student shared that their takeaway was "to put myself out there and take care of myself to be able to give my 110 percent to my community." By teaching students how to better respond to stress, we can inspire more empathetic, mindful, and aware leaders.

## Phase 6.3: Embody. Mindful Eating

**Timeframe:** 10 minutes

**Materials:** pieces of fruit, chocolate, or some other kind of food; video at www.youtube.com/@StressWisePractices-wo3kv

Follow the link to play the audio practice or read from the following script, then proceed with the activity that follows.

Find a comfortable seated position, and have the item of food you will be using nearby. [Pause.]

Take a few seconds to get really comfortable in your seat. Plant your feet on the ground. Try to lengthen up through your spine so you are sitting up tall, or leaning against a chair or wall if you need support. [Pause.]

Take a moment to notice how your body feels right now. [Pause.]

How is your breath? [Pause.]

How is your body temperature? [Pause.]

Are you hungry? [Pause.] If so, how do you know? [Pause.]

Now, go ahead and hold your item of food. Imagine this is your first time ever seeing this item! What do you notice about its color? [Pause.]

What do you notice about its texture? [Pause.]

Are there any details about this food item that are pleasing to you? [Pause.]

Did any sensations in your body change? Are you hungry? If so, how do you know? [Pause.]

Now you can bring this item up to your nose and notice the smell of it. Is the scent pleasant or unpleasant?

Does it change any sensations in your body?

Does it remind you of any memories? [Pause.]

What about the texture—what do you notice about how it *feels* to hold this item? [Pause.]

Using all your senses to get to know this mystery food item, what can you sense about it? How does it affect your body? [Pause.]

Now, we will take a bite of this food item. As you do, really savor the flavor of it. Notice the consistency. Swallow slowly and notice how it feels as this food item travels down in your digestion.

Pause before the next bite.

Did anything change in your body? Was it pleasant or unpleasant? Are you hungry? If so, how do you know?

If you would like to take another bite, you can do that now. Slowly savoring the flavor, noticing the texture, chewing slowly.

You can continue for a few more minutes, really getting to know how this food interacts with your body.

## Phase 6.4: Expand. Food Mood

**Timeframe:** 20 minutes

Read the following script aloud or invite a volunteer to do so:

The foods we eat are the building blocks of our energy, mood, immunity, and so much more. The enteric nervous system is created of 200 to 600 million neurons in the digestive tract called our "gut-brain," indicating the importance our digestive tract has on our mood. If you've ever experienced butterflies in your stomach or feeling sick to your stomach during a heartbreak or loss, you've had a direct experience of the gut-brain working. When we feed our digestive tracts whole foods that are grown locally and are in season, the microbiome becomes more able to transmit sensations of well-being, creates greater immunity, and sends nutrients to all organs, muscles, and bones (Huberman, 2022). When we eat foods that are highly processed, our mood and overall health can be negatively affected because we do not receive the variety of nutrients our bodies need to function optimally. The strength of our digestion is directly related to the way we interact with stress. When our digestion is nourished and functioning well, we are resilient and able to withstand stress with vitality. However, when digestion is limited, we become more reactive, which can lead to a greater sense of anxiety, depression, anger, frustration, and feeling overwhelmed by stressors.

Foods that are fresh, locally sourced, and in season are the best for digestion, and eating more fruits and vegetables is one of the single most effective things you can do to increase health. Though not all people have access to these resources, there are some simple things you can do to encourage digestion. Starting the day with a hot cup of water begins the digestive process (called peristalsis) and helps to stoke metabolism. Drinking water instead of soda during the day promotes hydration, encourages better nutrient absorption, and leads to fewer blood-sugar spikes (which means less mood swings). Trying a plant-based diet one day a week can also be beneficial, because it offers us a wider variety of vitamins and minerals that we get when we eat fruits and vegetables of every color. Try "eating the rainbow" by including green, purple, red, and yellow vegetables when you have the chance, to support better physical and mental health.

In addition to eating healthy food, we should space our meals out by three to four hours and try to avoid eating three hours or so before bed to give our digestive system a rest (Lad, 2012).

We may not always have access to the highest-quality foods, but when we start to learn about how important our digestion is, it will empower us to make different decisions when we can. Changing our eating habits is integral to our health as a society, and every opportunity we can take to eat more fruits and vegetables benefits us as a collective.

## Phase 6.5: Express. Stress-Wise Resource Survey

**Timeframe:** 10 minutes

Share this survey with students:

1. Are you aware of stress in your body, mind, or heart right now?
   __Y __N
2. If yes, what type(s) of stress do you detect? Select all that apply:
   __ Eustress
   __ Distress
   __ Tolerable stress
   __ Intolerable stress
   __ Chronic stress
   __ Acute stress
3. Are you aware of vitality in your body, mind, or heart right now?
   __Y __N
4. List a few sources of vitality for you:

   _____

   _____

   _____

5. Name at least one way you discharge stress in a stress-wise way:

    _____

    _____

6. What specific choices can you make to contribute to your own peace and well-being this week?

    _____

    _____

This qualitative self-assessment gauges students' awareness of stress and vitality in their lives. Cultivating awareness is the first step to stress intelligence and is threaded throughout the entire stress-wise framework. Regularly checking in with the quality of our awareness is a fundamental practice. In the beginning of awareness-based practices, it's common for adolescent students to find the topic confounding. However, over time and with practice, students will begin to understand the power of their awareness to shape their lives. When students learn to utilize their awareness as a gauge, they gain access to one of the powerful tools of the mind. Awareness itself is a resource.

The example of Jose, a 7th grade student, illustrates this process clearly.

When Jose was first introduced to awareness through mindful practice, he was resistant. He would roll his eyes and try his best to recruit classmates into his resistance. With a healing-centered approach, his teacher let him know that participation was a choice but that purposefully distracting classmates was not. She encouraged Jose to keep an open mind. Within six weeks of practice, Jose had gingerly started to engage, and by week eight he was a confident, willing practitioner.

One day, Jose asked his teacher if he could speak with her after class.

"The awareness showed me that playing Fortnite too much was making me more angry and stressed, so I cut my time in half and I feel a lot better now," he proudly shared.

This is how awareness works to boost our stress intelligence. It slowly seeps into our daily lives and begins to illuminate what is working for us and what is not. The key is consistent practice and engagement with awareness.

The final question in the survey is an opportunity for students to reflect on their agency to make wise choices. Consider which responses might be appropriate to integrate into your classroom over the next few weeks. Also, encourage students to share their responses with their caregivers, families, or other people they live with. For example, if a student identifies "time in nature" as a source of well-being, their family may plan for them to spend a day outdoors.

Although the focus of this book is on developing a stress-wise classroom, taking these insights, practices, and behaviors beyond the classroom expands the container in which your student can express their stress-wise skills and create a lifestyle that is based in self-respect and health. Whenever possible, remind students to apply what they are learning about stress and vitality outside the classroom walls. When students make the move to connect with their caregivers, family members, and friends with stress intelligence, well-being grows on a cultural level.

Educators' own well-being is a key factor in our capacity to help students cultivate stress IQ. With this in mind, consider which resources are most nourishing to you. What body-mind-heart resources do you need more of? Are you more supported by a breathing practice or a walk outdoors? As your own stress intelligence grows, your students will benefit by observing you modeling it. As you gain deeper insights into the kinds of resources that are most supportive for you and your students, is there anyone you feel compelled to share this information with? Would a colleague or an administrator benefit from knowing what is working for your class? Can you carry this information into your out-of-school relationships?

The next chapter explores the utility of relationships in developing a stress-wise classroom culture through social awareness.

# 7

# Relate: A Stress-Wise Classroom Culture

*As a classroom community, our capacity to generate excitement is deeply affected by our interest in one another, in hearing one another's voices, in recognizing one another's presence.*

— bell hooks

**Guiding Question**

How can educators help students utilize their stress intelligence to have a positive impact in school and apply their learning to their home and community lives?

The learning cycles in this chapter bring students into project-based learning to build social awareness, practice perspective-taking, and discover details about collective stressors. This work is specifically geared toward students' empowerment and agency in making shifts within classroom and campus climate and culture.

**From Abby's Classroom**

One of the first times I facilitated a stress-wise activity with high schoolers, the principal told me beforehand that this particular class had a "culture problem." Indeed, I discovered a class of 25 peers with very little positive interpersonal connection. There were racial tensions as well as a pronounced sense of competition and animosity among the female students. A biracial, transgender classmate found himself in the middle of what he described as a "mean mix of unhappy people." I was unsure if my multidisciplinary curriculum of social-emotional learning and mindful practices would be effective with this class.

One theme immediately stood out to me about these students: namely, that they were stressed on many levels and this was not being addressed. I decided to focus on one thing all students could relate to by asking, "Who here feels like they have too much stress in their life?" Every hand shot up instantly, accompanied by a concert of voices: "Me." "Yeah, that's me, too." "For sure." "Every day." "You know it, Miss." Students looked around and laughed together. The ice was broken.

Next, I asked, "How many of us know how to deal with stress in ways that feel healthy?" A few hands cautiously went up. Most students had confused and reflective looks on their faces. I let them know that my job was to help them work together to uncover their collective sources of stress and find some new ways to cope.

Over the course of seven sessions of interpersonal relationship building through activities focused on values, needs, goals, support, obstacles, stress, and coping, the students in this class discovered that their similarities outweighed their differences. The female students realized they had a choice to serve as either supports or obstacles for one another and were explicit in their new understanding that they were, as one student put it, "in it together." Students who had hardly looked each other in the eye for months began to build relationships founded on social awareness. These relationships transformed their perspectives to the point that group tension turned into classroom connection. Perhaps most affirming of all, the student who had felt like he was stuck in a "mean mix of unhappy people" responded in the final student evaluation with these words: "I'm so glad we got a chance to see how we can make all the difference to each other." After our final session, he shared with me that he finally felt like he belonged somewhere.

# Stress and Vitality Are Collective

*Through relationship we humanize one another, which is essential to preventing and ceasing the violence and hatred across difference.*

—Jacoby Ballard

In many sectors of society, chronic stress is accepted as an untamable part of our lives that we must tolerate to be successful—or worse, as a symbol of productivity and success. Stress management is a billion-dollar industry, yet stress remains a top contributor to many leading causes of death and disease. Perhaps this is because we too often direct individuals to manage stress on their own, in an isolated fashion. Of course, nothing and no one truly exists in isolation, so when stress permeates systems, a systemic approach to stress relief is needed. Understanding how stress impacts the people we live and work with is key to developing pragmatic stress intelligence. As we become more aware of how stress impacts society as a whole, we can see that personal stress management plans alone can only do so much.

When we plant only one type of plant in a garden, that garden is likely to suffer from disease or need chemical intervention. But when we plant a variety of plants that grow together, they cocreate a resilience that strengthens and protects the garden. Our hope is that students and educators alike will come to experience the inextricable connections between self and social awareness by leaning into the potential of coregulation.

Stress intelligence is not about "fixing" students, because our students are not broken. Judging the symptoms of a problem as the problem itself is myopic and ultimately unhelpful. Our students are adapting within a deficient system, and their stress functions as an indicator of the need for change and resolution. Too often, our education system ignores the neuroscientific and psychological complexities of learning while penalizing students for attempting to meet their basic human needs for connection and belonging (Padamsee, 2011). Schools that most effectively nurture student health are committed to recognizing and transforming the policies and practices eroding well-being in the first place. Chris

Emdin makes this point when he asks, "When will we recognize that even mindfulness, socioemotional learning, and restorative practices, *if nested in the perception that the youth are broken,* will only serve to maintain the existing structure?" (2021, pp. 157–158, emphasis added).

To transform the structural and systemic factors that perpetuate incomplete stress cycles, we must create a culture of care with practices nested in connection, compassion, and criticality. Educators who spend time on effective well-being practices break down two of the most pernicious misconceptions in unhealthy systems: that there is not enough time for health and that health is extracurricular. To cultivate stress intelligence is to tap into the wisdom of what is possible by taking a wide-angle view of what is sustainable across systems and what is necessary for the healthiest outcomes.

Body-mind-heart practices focused on building stress intelligence can contribute to the overall health of teens. The Centers for Disease Control and Prevention (2021) names youth and school connectedness as a significant protective factor that carries forward into adulthood. The project-based learning activities in this chapter are designed to strengthen youth and school connections in several critical ways. First, students develop deeper feelings of connection to one another as they become more aware of their commonalities and shared struggles. Then, the focus can shift to creating healthy school connections as students work together to positively influence school culture and climate. Students who feel they have a positive role to play in shaping their school environment feel more represented and invested in school, which has implications on how they will show up in other communities beyond the school, including their neighborhood, college, family, and work.

## Social Dimensions of Stress Intelligence

*Mindfulness is not just an individual practice, it is a collective movement towards well-being for all. We see our mindfulness as a tangible and vital response to injustice. It's the inner work that makes the outer work possible.*

—Dr. Sara King

The activities in this chapter encourage students to consider how stress affects the lives of their peers, families, and community members. The social implications of stress are explored in the context of the collective. Learning cycles aim to cultivate social awareness and compassion for others as well as considering the macrosystemic and socioeconomic implications of stress.

As you proceed through the learning cycles, we encourage you to look for and teach to connection. Allow your knowledge of your students and your own felt sense of what is working to guide the way. Remember that none of the content in this book needs to be executed exactly as written; the work of building mindfulness through stress intelligence is most effective when you incorporate your own creativity.

## Learning Cycle 1: Interconnectivity

**Objectives**
- Identify topics related to collective well-being within students' bioecological systems.
- Cultivate a stress-wise group culture through the cogeneration of values, needs, support, and obstacles.
- Nurture an embodied experience of peer connection.
- Investigate interconnection in the natural world.

**Outcomes**
- Students will become more socially attuned.
- Students will consider the interconnectivity of individual and collective well-being.

**Keywords:** *interconnection, collective*

### Phase 1.1: Engage. Ecology of Care and Connection

**Timeframe:** 20 minutes

**Materials:** Figure 7.1

Draw a large version of the bioecological model in Figure 7.1 on the board. Briefly explain that human development occurs within all six of the bioecological zones shown in the image.

## Figure 7.1. Bioecological Model

Starting from the outer circle and moving in toward the center, ask students to generate topics of care for each zone (e.g., "What topics related to stress and vitality stand out to you when you think about life online?"). Write or call on volunteers to write the topics in the given circles. Allow two to three minutes per zone for topics to emerge. Pause when you reach the center zone.

**Intrapersonal Check-In** (2–3 minutes)
Follow this script with your class:

> Take a moment to pause and check in with yourself. How is your body feeling at the moment? How is your mind? What words or phrases would you use to describe your inner state of being right now?

Now think back to the topics we generated together using the concentric circles. Imagine yourself at the center. Consider that the five circles around you represent the collective, or the world around you. When you consider your own well-being, what topics from the outer circles matter the most to you? Is there a particular outer circle you are most drawn to learn more about right now? [Pause for a few moments of reflection.]

Next, students choose one of the bioecological zones as their focus for research into special topics of care. Dedicate a different part of the classroom to each zone and direct students to assemble in their chosen one.

Help students form their new cohorts. Group sizes can vary, but if any zone has more than five students, divide them into multiple groups. Zones can also be combined. If a zone has only one student, invite others to join that zone or help that student connect to another zone while assuring them their topic of care will be included. Make note of the new groupings. Students will remain with these new groupings, or cohorts, for the remainder of the activities in the book.

## Phase 1.2: Explore. Where We Belong

**Timeframe:** 20 minutes

**Intrapersonal Check-In**

Follow this script with your class:

Before we get into our groups, let's take a moment to check in with ourselves. Consider what qualities might help you as we enter small-group work today. What would support you in being a supportive collaborator with your peers today?

Enjoy several full breaths while you think about the kind of support you hope to receive from your classmates, and think about how you can bring that kind of support to yourself right now.

Before we complete this check-in, think of one quality you believe is important for all group members to remember to bring to small-group meetings.

### Small-Group Values and Collective Needs

Students gather with their newly formed small groups to discuss the following prompts:

- Name one quality you think is important for all group members to remember to bring to small-group meetings.
- What would help you to be a supportive collaborator with your peers in this group?
- What is needed to deepen our collective well-being? List 5–10 needs group members have in common.

## Phase 1.3: Embody. Wheel of Connection Visualization

**Timeframe:** 10 minutes

Prompt the small groups to gather in circles. Then, follow this script:

Place your body in a position that feels easy and comfortable, either sitting or standing. Steady your gaze down below the horizon or gently close your eyes. Feel the parts of your body in connection with the floor or seat. Bring your awareness to those connections, grounding and feeling the support of the ground or floor, the building, and the earth. Bring your attention to your center, feeling your own inner strength. Feel the length of your spine and extend the crown of your head upward toward the sky. Let your awareness begin to settle around your heart. Start to visualize a sphere of emerald-green light in the center of your chest, radiating in all directions around your body. [Pause.]

Now, tune in to the presence of your group members in this circle. Imagine that each classmate also holds a sphere of green light in their heart center. [Pause.]

With each breath in, imagine your green light grows brighter.

With each breath out, visualize your light shining forward toward the center of the circle.

Try this for five breaths. [Pause.]

Inhale; your light intensifies.

Exhale; you send a stream of green light toward the center of the circle. [Pause.]

Visualize the streams of light beaming from each group member like spokes on a wheel forming a hub in the middle. [Pause.]

Now, begin to send this emerald light to the right of your body toward your nearest classmate.

Imagine the light beaming from your classmate on the left to you. [Pause.]

Visualize green light circulating through your entire circle. [Pause.]

Now, reverse the flow. Begin to beam green light toward your classmate to the left. Feel the light your classmate on the right is sending. Visualize this green light circulating around the circle. [Pause.]

Now, center your awareness in your own heart again and imagine this green light connecting your circle in its circumference, as well as through the middle point. [Pause.]

Remember the group values and collective needs of your group. Generate those qualities along these lines of connection. Breathe and generate these qualities from yourself. [Pause.]

Now breathe and receive these qualities from your group mates. [Pause.]

Slowly allow the visualization to dissolve. Take your time bringing your awareness back to the room. [Pause.]

Feel your feet and seat. Sense the walls around you and the ceiling. [Pause.]

Slowly flicker your eyes open if they are closed. Lift your gaze.

Allow groups a couple of minutes to share informally about their experience in this practice.

## Phase 1.4: Expand. Networks of Connection

**Timeframe:** 5–10 minutes

Follow this script with your class:

Did you know that when you are walking through a forest, you are walking on a vast and unseen network of communication between trees and plants? Beneath the soil, leaves, and ground, an extensive system of mycelium is interwoven with tree roots. This mycelium connects individual plants together to transfer water, nitrogen, carbon, and other minerals.

Mycelia are the tiny threads that wrap around and attach to tree roots, creating a network that can span the entire floor of a forest—you might call mycelium the "wood wide web." Through the mycelium, trees share nutrients and even communicate. Amazingly, approximately 90 percent of all land-based plants are connected in this way. (Perry, 2022)

Next, ask students these questions:
- If land-based plants are interconnected, do you think it is possible that humans are also interconnected?
- What are some ways you can imagine humans being connected?
- Why do you think it is important that plants are able to communicate and share nutrients with each other?
- What can we learn about interconnection from the "wood wide web"?

## Phase 1.5: Express. Collective Supports and Obstacles

**Timeframe:** 20 minutes

**Materials:** paper and writing utensils

**Layers of Support**

Students join their small groups in a circle for this brief body-mind-heart practice. Then, follow this script with your class:

You may sit or stand for this practice with your eyes closed or half-closed. Allow your body to settle, moment by moment, as you guide your attention to the parts of your body touching the ground or chair. Pause to feel those points of contact. [Pause.]

Focus on the solid feeling of the chair or the floor beneath you. Now, think about what is supporting the floor, the foundation of the building you are in. [Pause.]

Think about the ground beneath this building supporting the foundation. [Pause.]

Think about all the layers of support that exist beneath us, the layers of the Earth going all the way down to the core. Allow your body to rest into that support. [Pause.]

Now, bring your attention to the support that is all around us: the walls, the ceiling, the air, and the sun that give us life. [Pause.]

Let your body and mind feel and acknowledge all the support that surrounds us. I am here to support you. You are supporting each other. [Pause.]

Before coming back to the group, remember your group values from Phase 1.2 and bring them into your work today as support. [Pause.]

Slowly bring your awareness back to the room and the people around you. Share one word with your group to describe your experience in this practice.

**Naming Support and Obstacles**

Each group needs a sheet of paper (larger is better) in the center of their circle. Students write "Support" in the middle and fill in responses to the questions below, writing them all around the centered word.

- Who are the people in our lives who support us in meeting our collective needs?
- What activities and behaviors do we engage in that support our well-being?
- What mindsets and attitudes support us?
- How can we support one another?

Next, students flip over the sheet of paper and write "Obstacles" in the middle. All around this centered word, students write their answers to the following questions:

- What are the main obstacles we can see to our collective well-being?
- What behaviors or habits get in the way of our well-being?
- What ways of thinking get in our way?
- Are there any things we do that put us in one another's way?
- Bonus question: What is your group's mycelium?

To end this activity, have one member from each group share their findings with the large group.

Remind students to look for support every day. Also remind them that stress and vitality coexist, and though obstacles are sometimes easier to see than support is, when we meet obstacles with support in mind, we can overcome anything.

# Learning Cycle 2
# IRL Stress-Wise Application

**Objectives**
- Vote to select special topics of care for small groups to delve into through a stress-wise lens.
- Contemplate and relate with one another on the topic of collective resilience.
- Deepen knowledge of interconnection through engagement with scientific evidence involving the heart, mind, and breathing.
- Investigate stress intelligence as a resource for collective resilience using student creativity, life experiences, and language.

**Outcomes**
- Students will apply their stress intelligence to real-life situations.
- Students will have an amplified sense of awe at the nature of interconnectivity.

**Keyword**: *collective resilience*

## Phase 2.1: Engage. Zone in on Special Topics

**Timeframe:** 20 minutes

Remind students of the activity from Phase 1.1, where they used the bioecological model to choose a zone to focus on. Students now generate new topic possibilities with a fresh brainstorm, writing all ideas into a list.

Once the list is complete, it is passed around to each group member for a vote. Each member has three votes that they cast by putting a checkmark next to their top three topics. The three topics with the most votes go through an additional round of votes, with each member casting two votes this time. The topic with the most votes wins.

Each group discusses and records answers to the following prompts:

- What words or phrases would you use to describe how you feel about your group's topic right now?
- Why is this topic important to the group?
- Make a list of burning questions about your topic.

## Phase 2.2: Explore. Stress and Vitality Are Collective

**Timeframe:** 20 minutes

**Brainstorm** (5–7 minutes)

In their groups, students brainstorm their thoughts on the following prompt: "What are the stressors associated with your group's topic?" They then write down as many sources of stress as they can think of in relation to their topic. For example, if a group's topic is social media, students brainstorm all the ways using social media can be stressful for them and for youth in general.

**Practice: Breathing Is Life Support** (5 minutes)

Follow this script with your class:

> Notice how your body feels right after thinking about stress. Since we have been focusing on our shared stress, let's pause to remember our shared goal. Place your body in an upright, steady position. Feel the ground beneath us. [Pause.]
>
> Steady your gaze or close your eyes. Breathe in the air that is all around us. [Pause.]
>
> Now, imagine that each breath is an opportunity to support your group's shared goal. [Pause.]
>
> Remember the sources of support your group named. [Pause.]
>
> Think of one way of being or one behavior that your group decided could support you in reaching your goal. With each breath in, consider that you can breathe in not only oxygen but also support. [Pause.]

> Let your breath support you. Imagine your breath is like an anchor, helping to steady your mind. [Pause.]
>
> Follow each breath in, saying to yourself, "support." [Pause.]
>
> With each breath out, feel the support of the earth beneath you. [Pause.]
>
> Try this for five breaths. Then, slowly bring your awareness back to the room.

**Brainstorm** (5–7 minutes)

Students brainstorm and record their thoughts on the following prompt: "What role does your chosen topic play in collective vitality?" For example, if the group's topic is social media, students brainstorm how social media sources can connect youth to one another for organizing and inspiration.

## Phase 2.3: Embody. Resilience Is Collective

**Timeframe:** 20 minutes

**Reflections on Resilience** (5 minutes)

Guide students through this simple mindful breathing practice that leads into a reflection on collective resilience:

> Begin to bring your awareness closer to you. Pause to notice the parts of your body that are in connection with the floor or chair. [Pause.]
>
> Close or half-close your eyes. Notice your breath. For a few moments, simply observe each inhale and exhale. [Pause.]
>
> Slowly begin to deepen each inhale. Feel the breath bring a sense of softness to the inside of your body. [Pause.]
>
> Imagine each inhale is like a river carving its way through dense earth. Feel how your body can expand from inside during the inhale. [Pause.]
>
> Begin to lengthen each exhale, softening muscular tension in your shoulders, neck, and face. [Pause.]
>
> Keep breathing and softening for one minute. [Pause.]

Now, think about a time when you were part of a group that overcame a challenge. This could be a sports team, a community, or your family. [Pause.]

How did the group find the strength to meet the challenge? [Pause.]

What inner resources or character traits did the members of the group bring to help the group work through stress? [Pause.]

Where did the group's resilience come from? [Pause.]

Can you think of a time in history when humans survived a tragedy or overcame a serious challenge as a species? [Pause.]

Where does the resilience of humanity come from? What makes us resilient in the face of constant stress? [Pause.]

Slowly start to bring your awareness back to the room and the space around you. Take a few moments to look around and reorient yourself to the outside world.

**Sharing Success and Resilience** (15 minutes)

In their groups, students share stories of resilience from the preceding reflection. Then, ask students to discuss how resilience connects to their topics:

- In thinking about your topic, how is resilience important?
- What can be done to bolster resilience?

For example, if a group's topic is friendships, the group discusses ways in which resilience is important to healthy friendships. Then, the group focuses on how to nurture resilience in friendships.

When all groups are finished, a representative from each group shares a highlight with the whole class.

## Phase 2.4: Expand. Everything Is Connected

**Timeframe:** 20 minutes

Play the video "Everything Is Connected—Here's How" by Tom Chi (2016) for students (available here: www.youtube.com/watch?v=rPh3c8Sa37M). Then, choose to facilitate a discussion or have students journal using the following prompts:

- Did anything Tom Chi say surprise you?
- What part of the talk was most compelling to you?

## Phase 2.5: Express. Gestures of Resilience

**Timeframe:** 20 minutes

This is a student-led practice. In their small groups, students discuss and list the kinds of attitudes, behaviors, and attributes that contribute to resilience, then narrow the list down to two words. Next, students practice "breathing resilience" together for three minutes by thinking of one of the two words on each inhale and the other on each exhale. While thinking about these words, students try to breathe the qualities in and out.

After the breathing practice, students design gestures to depict their two chosen words. The gestures can use just the hands or the whole body. For example, a group that chooses *patience* and *perseverance* as their words may come up with lacing their fingers together in front of their bellies for *patience* and a swipe of the forehead for *perseverance*. When they are finished, groups share the gestures they designed with the whole class.

Encourage students to use these gestures as reminders of their personal and collective resilience.

# Learning Cycle 3
# Wisdom Is Power

**Objectives**
- Devise group statements and slogans on stress intelligence.
- Create posters to culminate learning with creative application of stress intelligence to be shared schoolwide.
- Contemplate the role of curiosity and compassion in conflict resolution.

**Outcomes**
- Students will cogenerate attunement strategies to restore peace.
- Students will share expressions of stress intelligence in kinship with the school community.

**Keywords:** *attunement, kinship*

## Phase 3.1: Engage. Collective Wisdom

**Timeframe:** 20 minutes

Each group devises a collective statement on stress and vitality using this prompt:

> Imagine you are creating a campaign for a more stress-wise school. Your group's goal is to communicate to your peers your knowledge on thriving through stressful challenges. In two to five sentences, capture the most important aspects of stress intelligence that you think your peers need to know.

## Phase 3.2: Explore. Empowering Slogans

**Timeframe:** 20 minutes

Each group refines its collective statement into a slogan using this prompt: "Imagine you are designing a poster for your campaign. Whittle your statement down to a campaign slogan that will captivate your peers' attention."

## Phase 3.3: Embody
### Genuine Inquiry: Questions to Bring the Peace

**Timeframe:** 10 minutes

Call for a volunteer to read the following quote from Bonnie Badenoch (2018): "The room was very quiet with that familiar deepening that arrives when something is happening underneath, beyond the words." Then, ask students to recall a time when they experienced or witnessed conflict in the classroom. Ask them to consider how stress may have played a role in the situation. Give them several minutes for contemplation.

Next, ask, "What if you were to approach the conflict with curiosity and compassion? How can we tune in, or become attuned, to what might be happening beneath the surface? What could you inquire about with your classmates to ease tensions? Devise a question or statement that can be used as an attunement strategy to restore peace."

Give students time to devise questions, then invite them to share with the whole class. Consider posting these attunement strategies in the classroom as artifacts for future reference.

## Phase 3.4: Expand. Kinship: Broader Than Friendship

**Timeframe:** 10 minutes

Call for a student volunteer to read the following quote from Neil deGrasse Tyson aloud: "Accepting our kinship with everyone on Earth is not just solid science, it's also a soaring spiritual experience."

**Class Discussion**

Ask students:

- What does this quote mean to you?
- What is kinship?
- How can kinship contribute to stress intelligence?

## Phase 3.5: Express. Share the Power

**Timeframe:** 20 minutes (or more, or completed as a group homework assignment)

**Materials:** paper or posterboard, markers, pencils, or a digital platform for making graphics

Students create posters, either on paper or digitally, displaying their slogans. Display these posters around campus to inspire well-being for all students.

# Learning Cycle 4: A Stress-Wise Future

**Objectives**

- Summarize learning and plan for daily application of stress intelligence.
- Envision a resourced world of vitality.
- Compose "calls to action" for collective well-being.
- Locate organizations in the collective well-being network.

**Outcomes**

- Students will create artifacts to inspire ongoing integration of stress intelligence.
- Students will develop a network of organizational resources to support further investigation.

**Keywords:** *apply, envision*

## Phase 4.1: Engage. Daily Applications

**Timeframe:** 20 minutes

**Materials:** sticky notes or index cards, tape

Guide students to reflect on their experience with stress-wise praxis and to look for ways to apply their learning. Prompt them to think about what they have learned about stress, vitality, resilience, coping, and inner resources. Suggest looking back through journals for clues.

List students' responses to the following prompts on the board:

- Thinking back on the body-mind-heart practices and activities for developing stress IQ, what stands out to you as memorable?
- What useful information did you learn about stress?
- How about vitality?

Next, give students sticky notes or index cards and ask them to write responses to the following prompts (one per note or card):

- What practices or activities would you want us to continue in our classroom?
- How about in your life outside school?

Write the following times of day on the board. Ask students to use tape to apply their notes or cards by each space that applies.

- Morning before school
- At school
- After school
- Before bed
- Weekend

## Phase 4.2: Explore
### Dream into a Well World: A Stress-Wise Call to Action

**Timeframe:** 20 minutes

Ask students, "In your wildest dreams, how will your group's chosen topic be impacted when more people make a commitment to collective well-being?" Give them three minutes or so to contemplate. Then, have students join their groups to share ideas. After about five minutes of discussion, ask students to create a call to action that includes a specific action they want people to take now to bring their vision to reality. Tell them to think about who needs to hear the call. Ask, "How can you deliver your call to action?" For example, a group whose special topic is environmental justice might come up with the call to action "Lessen carbon emissions now" directed at the highest-polluting corporations. They may choose to send the message directly to those companies or post on social media and tag them. Or a group focused on nonviolence in their community might come up with "See the good in each other," directed at community members. This message might be posted in the community as a billboard or an ad on benches and buses.

## Phase 4.3: Embody. Stress-Wise World Meditation

**Timeframe:** 20 minutes

**Materials:** video at www.youtube.com/@StressWisePractices-wo3kv

Follow the link to play the audio practice or read the following script, then proceed with the activity that follows.

> Find a comfortable position for your body, either seated or standing. Relax your eyes or close them. For a few moments, let your body settle into position. Notice the sensation of gravity drawing your body toward the Earth. [Pause for 10 seconds or more.]
>
> Notice the parts of your body that are in contact with the Earth or with the chair that is supported by the ground. Count your points of contact with the Earth. Choose one point that feels most anchored or steady to gently hold your attention for a few breaths. [Pause.]
>
> Now, begin to notice the length of your spine from your lower back all the way up to where your neck meets your skull. See if you can find a subtle lift and extension through your spine toward the sky. Imagine you are wearing a hat connected to a gigantic helium balloon that is floating the crown of your head up toward the sky.
>
> Inhale, extending your spine and crown upward.
>
> Exhale, grounding your feet or seat downward. [Pause.]

Try this for a few breaths, then see if you can find your body grounding and uplifting simultaneously, connecting Earth and sky. [Pause.]

Now, begin to visualize yourself and your group thriving into the world. Imagine your group doing your work to contribute to collective well-being. You know how to navigate the stress and obstacles. Your vitality is strong. What do you see? [Pause.]

Next, imagine the other groups in our class thriving into the world. See them moving through challenges with awareness and discernment, able to resource themselves. What do you see? [Pause.]

Now, visualize a world of people who know how to resource themselves and support one another in being well. What does a stress-wise world look like to you? [Pause.]

Slowly bring your awareness back to your anchor points with the Earth. Feel your spine uplifted to the sky. Notice the air touching your skin. Notice the room around you. Look around the room and notice one new thing you had not noticed before.

**Optional Activities**
- Brief journaling period to record any thoughts or visions from the practice
- Dyad, triad, or group sharing session
- Whole-class sharing circle

## Phase 4.4: Expand. Community Connections

**Timeframe:** 20 minutes or more

This is a student-led activity. In their groups, students conduct research to find one or two organizations that support well-being related to their special topics. Students then record the organization's name, location, mission, and contact information. Each group shares the organization and their rationale for choosing it with the whole class.

## Phase 4.5: Express. We Are Stress Wise

**Timeframe:** 20 minutes

In their groups, students take the following survey. Consider using Google Forms or another convenient format for collecting responses:

1. Are we aware of stress in our classroom currently? __Y __ N
2. If yes, what type(s) of stress are here? Choose all that apply:
   __ Eustress
   __ Distress
   __ Tolerable stress
   __ Intolerable stress
   __ Chronic stress
   __ Acute stress
3. What do we think the sources of stress are? List them:
   _____
   _____
   _____

4. Are we aware of vitality in our class? __Y __ N
5. Can we identify any sources of vitality for our class? If so, list them:
   _____
   _____
   _____

6. How can our group have a positive influence on the well-being of our class as a whole? What specific choices can we make to contribute to peace here?
   _____
   _____
   _____

7. Name two or three resources we would like our class to use to develop stress IQ. Record the resources as a drawing, meme, graphic, or list.

This final self-assessment is a relational process through each mode of the stress-wise framework:

- Questions 1 and 4 bring students into connection with their awareness, to **know** if stress and/or vitality is present.
- Question 2 asks students to **differentiate** between the kinds of stress they are experiencing.
- Questions 3 and 5 lead students to **identify** stressors and sources of vitality.

- Question 6 guides students to **discern** how their group will contribute to classroom culture.
- Question 7 centers on **resourcing**.

This survey can be repeated on a regular basis or any time you feel students can benefit from a stress-wise check-in. Giving students this opportunity to **relate** on their well-being will deepen their coregulation skills over time. Each group should share its findings with the whole class. Consider using the documentation from question seven as artifacts in your classroom reminding the groups of their capacity to coregulate.

## Onward, Together

*Never give children a chance of imagining that anything exists in isolation. Make it plain from the very beginning that all living is relationship. Show them relationships in the woods, in the fields, in the ponds and streams, in the village and in the country around it. Rub it in.*

—Aldous Huxley

We hope the LCs in this chapter serve to create stronger, healthier interpersonal connections in your classroom. Becoming stress wise *requires* us to consider one another. Our actions impact others, and vice versa. When we approach well-being from a collective standpoint, we can start to take responsibility for the stress we may cause other people as well as realize that we have options in how we navigate stress imposed upon us. Developing stress intelligence is a lifelong process akin to other aspects of human development, like learning to communicate effectively. We encourage you to shape the ongoing process in a way that feels authentic and meaningful to you. This might look like any of the following:

- Integrating body-mind-heart practices on a regular basis
- Adopting a consistent habit of checking in on students' stress levels
- Becoming attuned to your students' humanity and allowing the learning process to flow from a sense of care and compassion

# Final Considerations

We encourage you to find some time to rest and reflect on your experience with the stress-wise framework. What parts stand out to you as the most supportive and meaningful for your class? What is your intention going forward with lessons for cultivating stress intelligence? Has your intention to focus on stress intelligence changed over time or remained mostly steady? What have you learned about yourself and your students in this process? These kinds of reflections are vital to the process of integrating stress intelligence into the landscape of your classroom culture and normalizing a more holistic dimensionality among and with your students. Your unique responses can guide your way forward with this work.

Perhaps there are certain activities or practices that simply didn't fit your teaching style or meet your students' specific needs. That's OK! You have full license to apply your knowledge and creativity—to modify the content of this book going forward in ways that serve you and your classroom more beautifully.

Remember: To stress is normal; to get wise about stress is extraordinary. We have witnessed the transformative power of body-mind-heart practices in schools for decades and are deeply grateful for each and every educator who continues to center their students' health and well-being within the educational process.

# Bibliography

American Foundation for Suicide Prevention. (2022). *Suicide statistics*. Author. https://afsp.org/suicide-statistics

André, C. (2019, January 15). Proper breathing brings better health. *Scientific American*. www.scientificamerican.com/article/proper-breathing-brings-better-health

Arao, B., & Clemens, K. (2013). From safe spaces to brave places: A new way to frame dialogue around diversity and social justice. In L. M. Landreman (Ed.), *The art of effective facilitation* (pp. 135–149). Stylus.

Archibald, J., Lee-Morgan, J. B., & De Santolo, J. (Eds.). (2019). *Decolonizing research: Indigenous storywork as methodology*. ZED Books.

Badenoch, B. (2018). *The heart of trauma: Healing the embodied brain in the context of relationships*. Norton.

Ballard, J. (2022). *A queer Dharma: Yoga and meditations for liberation*. North Atlantic Books.

Barbezat, D. P., & Bush, M. (2013). *Contemplative practices in higher education: Powerful methods to transform teaching and learning*. Wiley.

Batacharya, S., Wong, Y. R., & Ng, R. (2018). *Sharing breath: Embodied learning and decolonization*. AU Press.

Belenky, M. F. (1997). *A tradition that has no name: Nurturing the development of people, families, and communities*. Basic Books.

Benson, H. (1976). *The relaxation response*. William Morrow.

Birdsong, M. (2020). *How we show up: Building community in these fractured times*. Hachette Books.

Bluth, K. (2017, October 19). How to help teens become more self-compassionate. *Greater Good*. https://greatergood.berkeley.edu/article/item/how_to_help_teens_become_more_self_compassionate

Bordoni, B., Purgol, S., Bizzarri, A., Modica, M., & Morabito, B. (2018, June 1). The influence of breathing on the central nervous system. *Cureus, 10*(6). www.ncbi.nlm.nih.gov/pmc/articles/PMC6070065

Bronfenbrenner, U. (1992). Ecological systems theory. In R. Vasta (Ed.), *Six theories of child development: Revised formulations and current issues* (pp. 187–249). Jessica Kingsley.

Center for Healthy Minds. (n.d.). Research provides tools for achieving the "how" of well-being in daily life. https://centerhealthyminds.org/news/research-clues-in-on-the-how-of-emotional-health-in-daily-life

Centers for Disease Control and Prevention. (2019). Sleep and health. www.cdc.gov/healthyschools/sleep.htm

Centers for Disease Control and Prevention. (2021, July 22). Support for teens and young adults. www.cdc.gov/mentalhealth/stress-coping/teens-young-adults-support

Chi, T. (2016). Everything is connected—here's how. [Video]. TEDxTaipei. www.youtube.com/watch?v=rPh3c8Sa37M

Chrisinger, B. W., & Rich, T. (2020). Contemplation by design: Leveraging the "power of the pause" on a large university campus through built and social environments. *Frontiers in Public Health, 8*(31). doi:10.3389/fpubh.2020.00031

Collaborative for Academic, Social, and Emotional Learning (CASEL). (2022, January 5). CASEL: Advancing social and emotional learning. https://casel.org

Damour, L. (2019, August 10). Why stress and anxiety aren't always bad. www.apa.org/news/press/releases/2019/08/stress-anxiety

Dana, D. A. (2018). *Polyvagal theory in therapy.* Norton.

Dean, B. (2022). Vitality. *Authentic happiness.* www.authentichappiness.sas.upenn.edu/newsletters/authentichappinesscoaching/vitality

Desikachar, T. K. V. (1999). *The heart of yoga: Developing a personal practice.* Inner Traditions International.

Dewey, J. (1938/2015). *Experience and education.* Free Press.

Emdin, C. (2021). *Ratchetdemic.* Beacon Press.

Farb, N. A., Segal, Z., Mayberg, H., Bean, J., McKeon, D., Fatima, Z., & Anderson, A. (2007). Attending to the present: Mindfulness meditation reveals distinct neural modes of self-reference. *Social Cognitive and Affective Neuroscience, 2*(4), 313–322.

Garbarino, J. (2017). *Children and families in the social environment: Modern applications of social work.* Routledge.

Ginwright, S. A. (2021, October 7). Healing-centered engagement and the four pivots. Healing-Centered Education Summit, online.

Ginwright, S. A. (2022). *Four pivots: Reimagining justice, reimagining ourselves.* North Atlantic Books.

Goleman, D., & Davidson, R. J. (2017). *Altered traits: Science reveals how meditation changes your mind, brain, and body.* Avery.

Hanson, R. (2019, August 27). Confronting the negativity bias. www.rickhanson.net/how-your-brain-makes-you-easily-intimidated

Hess, R. S., & Copeland, E. P. (2001). Students' stress, coping strategies, and school completion: A longitudinal perspective. *School Psychology Quarterly, 16*(4), 389–405.

Holewinski, B. (n.d.). Underground networking: The amazing connections beneath your feet. National Forest Foundation. www.nationalforests.org/blog/underground-mycorrhizal-network

Hook, J. N., Davis, D. E., Owen, J., Worthington Jr., E. L., & Utsey, S. O. (2013). Cultural humility: Measuring openness to culturally diverse clients. *Journal of Counseling Psychology, 60*(3), 353–366.

hooks, b. (1994). *Teaching to transgress: Education as the practice of freedom.* Routledge.

hooks, b. (2013). *Teaching community: A pedagogy of hope.* Taylor & Francis.

Horton, M. (1990). *We make the road by walking: Conversation on education and social change.* Temple University Press.

Huberman, A. (2022, February 28). How to enhance your gut microbiome for brain and overall health. *Huberman Lab.* https://hubermanlab.com/how-to-enhance-your-gut-microbiome-for-brain-and-overall-health

Jensen, E. (1998). *Teaching with the brain in mind.* ASCD.

Johns Hopkins Medicine. (2019). What is Ayurveda? *Johns Hopkins Medicine.* www.hopkinsmedicine.org/health/wellness-and-prevention/ayurveda

Johns Hopkins Medicine. (2021, November 1). The brain-gut connection. www.hopkins medicine.org/health/wellness-and-prevention/the-brain-gut-connection

Johnson, M. (2021). *Finding refuge: Heart work for healing collective grief.* Shambhala.

Johnson, M. C., & Kelly, K. (2021, January–July). *Race and resilience (leadership cohort)* [Course]. www.raceandresilience.com

Khalaf, B. K., & Zin, Z. B. M. (2018). Traditional and inquiry-based learning pedagogy: A systematic critical review. *International Journal of Instruction, 11*(4), 545–564.

Khouri, H. (2021). *Peace from anxiety: Get grounded, build resilience, and stay connected amidst the chaos.* Shambhala.

Konturek, P. C., Brzozowski, T., & Konturek, S. J. (2011). Stress and the gut: Pathophysiology, clinical consequences, diagnostic approach and treatment options. *Journal of Physiology and Pharmacology, 62*(6), 591–599.

Krowiak, S. (2021, May 14). The vagus nerve: Your superhighway to physical, mental, and emotional health. www.tuneupfitness.com/blog/vagus-nerve

Lad, V. (2012). *Textbook of Ayurveda.* Ayurvedic Press.

Liu, Y. Z., Wang, Y. X., & Jiang, C. L. (2017). Inflammation: The common pathway of stress-related diseases. *Frontiers in Human Neuroscience, 11*, 316.

Love, B. (2019). *We want to do more than survive: Abolitionist teaching and the pursuit of educational freedom.* Beacon Press.

Magee, R. V. (2021). *The inner work of racial justice: Healing ourselves and transforming our communities through mindfulness.* TarcherPerigee.

McEwen, B. S. (2008). Central effects of stress hormones in health and disease: Understanding the protective and damaging effects of stress and stress mediators. *European Journal of Pharmacology, 583*(2–3), 174–185.

Nagoski, E., & Nagoski, A. (2020). *Burnout: The secret to unlocking the stress cycle.* Vermilion.

National Alliance on Mental Illness. (2022). Mental health by the numbers. www.nami.org/mhstats

National Institute of Mental Health. (2021). *I'm so stressed out!* Fact sheet. Author.

National Scientific Council on the Developing Child. (2004). *Young children develop in an environment of relationships.* (Working Paper No. 1).

National Scientific Council on the Developing Child. (2005/2014). *Excessive stress disrupts the architecture of the developing brain.* (Working Paper No. 3). Updated edition. www.developingchild.harvard.edu

Ndefo, N., & Glei, J. K. (Hosts). (2021, January 20). Coming home to yourself [Podcast episode]. *Hurry Slowly.*

Neff, K. (2020, July 9). Definition and three elements of self-compassion. https://self-compassion.org/the-three-elements-of-self-compassion-2

Neff, K. (2022). *Fierce self-compassion: How women can harness kindness to speak up, claim their power, and thrive.* Penguin Life.

Neff, K., & Germer, C. (2018). *The mindful self-compassion workbook: A proven way to accept yourself, build inner strength, and thrive.* Guilford Press.

Nestor, J. (2021). *Breath: The new science of a lost art.* Penguin.

Padamsee, Y. M. (2011, June 19). Communities of care, organizations for liberation. https://nayamaya.wordpress.com/2011/06/19/communities-of-care-organizations-for-liberation

Palmer, S. (1989). Occupational stress. *The Health and Safety Practitioner, 7*(8), 16–18.

Panda, S. (2020). *The circadian code: Lose weight, supercharge your energy, and transform your health from morning to midnight.* Rodale.

Paul, A. M. (2021). *The extended mind: The power of thinking outside the brain.* Houghton Mifflin Harcourt.

Perry, P. (2022, April 19). Plants and trees communicate through an unseen web. https://bigthink.com/surprising-science/plants-and-trees-communicate-help-each-other-and-even-poison-enemies-through-an-unseen-web

Peters, A., McEwen, B. S., & Friston, K. (2017). Uncertainty and stress: Why it causes diseases and how it is mastered by the brain. *Progress in Neurobiology, 156,* 164–188.

Porges, S. W. (2011). *The polyvagal theory: Neurophysiological foundations of emotions, attachment, communication, and self-regulation.* Norton.

Poynter, K. J., & Tubbs, N. J. (2008). Safe zones: Creating LGBT safe space ally programs. *Journal of LGBT Youth, 5*(1), 121–132.

Price, C. J., & Hooven, C. (2018). Interoceptive awareness skills for emotion regulation: Theory and approach of mindful awareness in body-oriented therapy (MABT). *Frontiers in Psychology, 9,* 798.

Rosenberg, S. (2017). *Accessing the healing power of the vagus nerve.* North Atlantic Books.

Ryan, R. M., & Frederick, C. (1997). On energy, personality, and health: Subjective vitality as a dynamic reflection of well-being. *Journal of Personality, 65,* 529–565.

Saccareccia, N. S. (2017). *Roadmap to mindful living.* Author.

Schwartz, A. (2017, March 25). Embodiment in somatic psychology. *Center for Resilience Informed Therapy.* https://drarielleschwartz.com/embodiment-in-somatic-psychology-dr-arielle-schwartz

Sefa Dei, G. J., & Kempf, A. (2006). *Anti-colonialism and education: The politics of resistance.* Sense Publishers.

Selye, H. (1956). *The stress of life.* McGraw-Hill.

Siegel, D. J. (1999). *The developing mind: Toward a neurobiology of interpersonal experience.* Guilford Press.

Siegel, D. J. (2007). *The mindful brain: Reflection and attunement in the cultivation of well-being.* Norton.

Siegel, D. J. (2013). *Brainstorm: The power and purpose of the teenage brain.* Jeremy P. Tarcher.

Simmons, D. (2021, March 21). Why SEL alone isn't enough. *Educational Leadership, 78*(6). www.ascd.org/el/articles/why-sel-alone-isnt-enough

Singh, A., & Suni, E. (2022, April 18). Technology in the bedroom. www.sleepfoundation.org/bedroom-environment/technology-in-the-bedroom

Strauss, C., Lever Taylor, B., Gu, J., Kuyken, W., Baer, R., Jones, F., & Cavanagh, K. (2016). What is compassion and how can we measure it? A review of definitions and measures. *Clinical Psychology Review, 47.*

Suldo, S. M., Shaffer, E. J., & Riley, K. N. (2008). A social-cognitive-behavioral model of academic predictors of adolescents' life satisfaction. *School Psychology Quarterly, 23*(1), 56–69.

Suni, E., & Truong, K. (2022, May 13). Sleep statistics: Facts and data about sleep. www.sleepfoundation.org/how-sleep-works/sleep-facts-statistics

Taylor & Francis Group. (2021, November 2). Lack of sleep affecting students' mental health, especially women: Daytime tiredness and sleep deprivation put students at risk of depression and high stress. *ScienceDaily.* www.sciencedaily.com/releases/2021/11/211102111148.htm

Tervalon, M., & Murray-Garcia, J. (1998). Cultural humility versus cultural competence: A critical distinction in defining physician training outcomes in multicultural education. *Journal of Health Care for the Poor and Underserved, 9,* 117–125.

Thayer, R. E. (1987). Energy, tiredness, and tension effects of a sugar snack versus moderate exercise. *Journal of Personality and Social Psychology, 52*(1), 119–125.

Tippett, K. (Host). (2021, December 2). Vivek Murthy and Richard Davidson: The future of well-being [Podcast episode]. *On Being.*

Tippett, K. (Host). (2022, February 3). Trabian Shorters: A cognitive skill to magnify humanity [Podcast episode]. *On Being.*

Treleaven, D. A., & Britton, W. (2018). *Trauma-sensitive mindfulness: Practices for safe and transformative healing.* Norton.

Tyson, N. D. (Host). (2014). *Cosmos: A spacetime odyssey.* [Documentary]. National Geographic Channel.

Vo, D. X. (2015). *The mindful teen: Powerful skills to help you handle stress one moment at a time.* New Harbinger.

Walker, M. (2017). *Why we sleep.* Scribner.

Wijeyakumar, A. (2021). *Meditation with intention: Quick and easy ways to create lasting peace.* Llewellyn.

# Index

The letter *f* following a page number denotes a figure.

acceptance, 143–144
accessibility, 14–16
acknowledgment, 26–27
adrenaline, 70
agency, 25
*ahimsa*, 13, 84–85
alternative activities, 15
animal breathing, 146–147
animal movement, 147–148
aptitudes, 29–30
aspirations, 29–30
assessment, 18–19
asset framing, 29–30
attributes, 29–30
autonomic nervous system, 55
awareness
    cultivating, 33–40
    definition, 35
    hidden power of, 24–25
    locating, 34–36
    mindful, 25–27
    stress cycles and, 69–70
    of stressors, 83–84
Ayurveda, 5–6

Badenoch, Bonnie, 170
Benson, Herbert, 133
bioecological model of human development, 159*f*
body-based practices. *See* physical (body-based) practices
body scanning, 34, 67, 97–98
boundaries, setting, 107–109, 115–116

breathing
    animal breathing, 146–147
    as resource, 130–134
*Breath: The New Science of a Lost Art* (Nestor), 132
bridge of self-awareness visualization, 88–89
*Burnout: The Secret to Unlocking the Stress Cycle* (Nagoski), 68

casual group, 16
centering, 43–45
centering yourself, 19
choice in practice, 15–16, 100–106
class discussions, 16
classroom culture
    about, 154–155
    stress IQ and, 3, 8–10
collective stress IQ, 3–4, 8–10
common humanity, 142
common humanity exercise, 82–83
community connections, 174
compassion
    common humanity and, 142
    exploring, 140–142
    self-compassion, 143–144
    self-compassionate touch, 142–143
    stress IQ and, 3
compliance, 12
conscious rest meditation, 136–138
constructivist approach, 8
contemplative approach, 8

coping, perception of skill of, 51
coping strategies, 77
COVID-19 pandemic, 74
critical approach, 8

decision making
    asking better questions, 102–103
    choosing wisest response, 100–102
    clear view visualization, 103
    discernment, 92–93, 99
    gut instincts, 110–112, 111*f*, 112*f*
    self-soothing practices, 109–110
    setting boundaries and finding help, 107–109
    somatic awareness and, 95–100
    voice of wisdom, 106–107
    Window of Well-Being, 103–106, 104*f*
de-escalation, 170
diagnostic assessment, 18
discernment, 92–93, 99
discussion facilitator role, 17
distress, 51, 53*f*, 54, 55

Emdin, Chris, 156–157
emotional IQ, 3, 26
emotional (heart-based) practices, 4–6, 5*f*
environment, stress and, 2
eustress, 51, 55
evaluation, 19
"Everything Is Connected—Here's How" (video), 168
exercise, 79, 88
exteroception, 38–40, 89
eye reset practice, 127–128

fight-or-flight, 111
5-2-6 Breathing Pattern Exercise, 133
food
    for energy, 99
    food mood, 150–151
    mindful eating, 148–149
    as pillar of health, 79, 88
formative assessment, 18

guided meditation, 34, 62
guiding body-heart-mind practices, 19–20

gut-brain axis, 112*f*
gut instincts, 110–112, 111*f*, 112*f*

habits, 2
healing-centered approach, 8
heart-based practices. *See* emotional (heart-based) practices
help, finding, 108–109
homeostasis, 23
human connection, stress IQ and, 8–10
hypothalamus, 55

intentional breathing, 134
interconnectivity
    collective supports and obstacles, 163–165
    "Everything Is Connected—Here's How" (video), 168
    networks of connection, 162–163
    resilience, 167–168, 169
    small-group values and collective needs, 161
    wheel of connection visualization, 161–162
internal resources
    bridge of self-awareness visualization, 88–89
    checking for understanding, 90–91
    common humanity exercise, 82–83
    coping strategies, 77
    food, sleep, and exercise, 79, 88
    sources of strength and wisdom, 80–85
    sources of vitality, 76–80
interoception, 38–40, 89

Johnson, Michelle Cassandra, 13
journals/journaling
    about, 18
    breathing, 134
    compassion, 144–145
    differentiating self from stress, 60
    harmless helpers, 85
    joy, 99–100
    "Potato, Egg, Coffee," 101–102
    rest and sleep, 140
    strengths and talents, 33
joy, 99–100

Khouri, Hala, 25
kinship, 171
knowing, ways of, 38–39

learning cycles
  cultivating awareness, 33–40
  gaining perspective on stress, 40–47
  stress-wise basics, 27–33
Love, Bettina, 3

materials, 17
meditation, 68–69, 136–138, 173–174
mental health disorders, 74
mental (mind-based) practices, 4–6, 5*f*
microbiome, 111*f*
mind-based practices. *See* mental (mind-based) practices
mindful awareness, 25–27, 62
mindful eating, 148–149
mindful practice effectiveness, 14
mindset, 1
mobilizing, 70
modulation, 33
mood, 66, 111, 112*f*, 139, 146, 150–151
movement, animal, 147–148
Murthy, Vivek, 85
music, for repose, 135–136

Nagoski, Amelia, 68
Nagoski, Emily, 68
naming, 26–27
nature and outdoors, 121
Nestor, James, 132
neuroception, 89
non-harming, 13, 84–85
notetaker role, 17

observation as participation, 15–16

pacing, 20
parasympathetic nervous system, 55, 56*f*
Paul, Annie Murphy, 121
pause, 20, 50–51, 57
*Peace from Anxiety* (Khouri), 25
pedagogical background of stress-wise praxis, 8
perception, and stress, 51, 125–127, 126*f*, 128–129

physical (body-based) practices, 4–6, 5*f*
polyvagal theory, 14
popcorn circle, 16
Porges, Stephen, 14
postural choice, 15
"Potato, Egg, Coffee," 101–102
praxis, 4, 32
productivity, 116

reaction to stress, 94–95
reflection, 47
relative safety, 13–14
relaxation, 34, 68–69
repetition, 21
repose
  checking for understanding, 140
  as form of boundary setting, 116
  playlist for, 135
  *versus* sleep, 135
resilience, 61–62, 167–168, 169
resourcing
  about, 115–118
  breathing, 130–134
  collective supports and obstacles, 163–165
  discharging stress and revitalizing vitality, 124–130
  draining the stress sink, 125–127, 126*f*
  eye and mind reset, 127–128
  matching resources with stressors, 119
  nature and outdoors, 121
  recharging vitality, 119–121, 120*f*
  resource inventory, 129–130
  resource survey, 151–153
  vagus nerve and, 121–123, 122*f*
response to stress, 94–95
rest
  checking for understanding, 140
  conscious rest meditation, 136–138
  repose playlist, 135–136
  repose *versus* sleep, 135
  science of sleep, 138–139
roles, in small groups, 17

safety, 13–14, 89
saying no, 107–108, 144
self-appreciation, 77–78

self-compassion, 143–144
self-compassionate touch, 142–143
self-efficacy, 3
self-soothing practices, 109–110
sensory awareness, 35–36, 38–40, 97–98
sequential circle, 16
Shorters, Trabian, 29
sleep
    checking for understanding, 140
    as pillar of health, 79, 88
    repose *versus,* 135
    science of, 138–139
    self-evaluation of, 93
small groups, 16–17, 161
social awareness, 3
somatic approach, 8
somatic awareness, 25, 95–100
strength, sources of, 80–85
strength-building, 30
stress
    chronic, 23–24, 156
    as collective, 156–157, 166–167
    definition, 23
    discharging, 124–130
    effects of, 1–2
    gaining perspective on, 40–47
    identity and, 60
    impact on growth, 58
    perception and, 51
    reaction *versus* response to, 94–95
    stress cycles, 49–50, 50*f,* 58–59, 63–64, 65–71, 157
    and vitality, 41–42, 52–54, 53*f,* 63–64, 65*f*
stress IQ
    basics of, 27–33
    checking for understanding, 45–46
    defined, 2
    definition, 32
    and human connection, 8–10
    integral to healthy classroom, 3
    mindfulness and, 25–27
    social dimensions of, 157–158
    within the system, 3–4
    vitality and, 24
stressors
    awareness of, 83–84
    identifying, 86–87, 87*f*
    matching with resources, 119

stress sink, draining the, 125–127, 126*f*
stress-wise framework
    about, 6–8, 7*f*
    accessibility, 14–16
    basics of, 27–33
    basic supports, 16–19
    choice, 15–16
    definition, 32
    final assessment, 174–176
    final considerations, 177
    implementation plans, 10–11
    liberation *versus* compliance, 12
    long-term commitment to, 12
    outcomes, 11–12
    safety considerations, 13–14
stress-wise praxis
    application IRL, 165–169
    basics of, 27–33
    call to action, 173
    checking for understanding, 113–114
    daily applications, 172
    definition, 32
    final assessment, 174–176
    overview, 4–6, 5*f*
    resource survey, 151–153
students
    mindful awareness in, 26
    supporting, 75–76, 78–79
student surveys, 19
summative assessment, 19
support, 75–76, 78–79, 107–110
supports and obstacles, collective, 163–165
sympathetic nervous system, 55, 56*f*
system, stress IQ within the, 3–4

teacher facilitators
    guiding body-heart-mind practices, 19–20
    individualizing approaches, 20–21
    reflection, 21, 47, 72, 91
thirst (sensory awareness), 36–37
thoughts, 124–125
timekeeper role, 17
touch, self-compassionate, 142–143
transformational approach, 8
transitions, 20
trauma sensitivity, 13–14

Treleaven, David, 14
Tyson, Neil deGrasse, 171

vagus nerve, 111, 121–123, 122*f*
visualizations
    bridge of self-awareness, 88–89
    stress-wise world, 173–174
    wheel of connection, 161–162
vitality
    as collective, 156–157, 166–167
    defining, 24
    discerning seed of, 93
    identifying sources of, 76–80
    recharging, 119–121, 120*f*, 124–130
    on spectrum, 4
    and stress, 41–42, 52–54, 53*f*,
        63–64, 65*f*

voice of wisdom, 106–107, 114
voice/prosody, 20

well-being, stress and, 3, 41–42
wheel of connection visualization,
    161–162
Window of Tolerance, 14
Window of Well-Being, 103–106, 104*f*
wisdom
    collective, 170
    empowering slogans, 170, 171
    investigating, 28
    restoring peace, 170
    sources of, 80–85
    stress IQ and, 4
    voice of, 106–107, 114
    wisdom shifts, 14, 30–31, 33

# About the Authors

**Abby Wills** is a mother, educator, and writer who has dedicated over 20 years to integrating healing-centered contemplative practices and courses for well-being into a wide diversity of public, charter, and private school settings through direct service to learners and educators throughout Los Angeles and internationally. Her work spans from early childhood education to university-based teacher education departments, with a strong focus on high schools serving targeted youth. She works closely with colleagues to codevelop programs in response to the collective needs, dreams, and cultures of learning communities.

Abby holds a bachelor's degree in human development with a specialization in developmental education and a master's in human development with a specialization in social change from Pacific Oaks College. As cofounder of Shanti Generation and Peace Lab projects, Abby develops digital and live curricula focused on mindful life skills for adolescents with a deep focus on embodied social-emotional learning and liberatory practices. In her role as movement, mindfulness, and social-emotional development specialist for Full Circle Consulting Systems, Abby facilitates professional development and training for K–12 educators and higher education faculty as well as support for parents and caregivers. She has earned multiple certifications in yoga, mindfulness, meditation, trauma-informed practice, and embodiment. Follow her on Instagram: @teachlovebreathe.

## About the Authors

**Anjali Deva** is an Ayurvedic practitioner and educator. Her private practice, Rooted Rasa, specializes in an integrative and trauma-informed approach to Ayurveda. Anjali is the founder of Mādhya Way, a school for Ayurveda. Her compassion-based approach is useful in alleviating anxiety, depression, PTSD, digestive disorders, and women's health issues using a holistic framework.

Anjali is greatly fortunate to have been introduced to Ayurveda and yoga at a young age by her father and mentor, Arun Deva. Her clinical experience began at Hope Integrative Psychiatry and was overseen by Omid Naim. Her familial lineage is rich with the desire to preserve and maintain these healing arts. Driven by her aspiration to better understand the connection between food and mood, she has trained with Kerala Ayurveda Academy, Loyola Marymount's Yoga and the Healing Sciences Program, and various teachers in both the United States and India. Her strong passion for digestion and mental health provides others with a holistic approach to finding their inner harmony and resilience for healing. Anjali is dedicated to sharing the Wisdom of Ayurveda for the benefit of all living beings. Learn more at rootedrasa.com and follow her on Instagram: @anjali.

**Niki Saccareccia** is the founder of Light Inside Yoga, which offers a therapeutic approach to wellness education. Since 2014, she has held the top credential in her field (E-RYT 500) and serves as a continuing education provider through the Yoga Alliance.

Niki has a background in behavioral psychology and spent her early career as a behavioral interventionist and clinical program manager. Niki's East-meets-West approach applies a unique blend of data-driven behavior change with the philosophical traditions of yoga in her private practice with individuals, groups, and corporate programs and in her classes, workshops, training, and retreats. She sits on the medical team at

Goodpath, an integrative, whole-person approach to pain management, and is a teacher on staff at Wellset.co, a digital holistic studio.

Niki is the author of *Roadmap to Mindful Living: A Practice Book for Turning Good Intentions into Long Term Habits* and the developer of a research-based curriculum for creating sustainable changes in well-being. Her pragmatic approach has been included at University of Southern California's Novus Think Tank, Loyola Marymount's master's degree program in yogic studies, Van Nuys Medical Magnet High School, and Pasadena City College in Southern California. Connect with her on social media @lightinsideyoga and at www.lightinsideyoga.com.

# Related ASCD Resources

At the time of publication, the following resources were available (ASCD stock numbers appear in parentheses).

*All Learning Is Social and Emotional: Helping Students Develop Essential Skills for the Classroom and Beyond* by Nancy Frey, Douglas Fisher, and Dominique Smith (#119033)

*Fostering Resilient Learners: Strategies for Creating a Trauma-Sensitive Classroom* by Kristin Van Marter Souers with Pete Hall (#116014)

*Mindfulness in the Classroom: Strategies for Promoting Concentration, Compassion, and Calm* by Thomas Armstrong (#120018)

*Powerful Student Care: Honoring Each Learner as Distinctive and Irreplaceable* by Grant A. Chandler and Kathleen M. Budge (#123009)

*Relationship, Responsibility, and Regulation: Trauma-Invested Practices for Fostering Resilient Learners* by Kristin Van Marter Souers with Pete Hall (#119027)

*Supporting Emotional Regulation in the Classroom* (QRG) by Jodi Place (#QRG121062)

*Teaching and Supporting Students Living with Adversity* (QRG) by Debbie Zacarian and Lourdes Alvarez-Ortiz (#QRG120035)

*Teaching to Strengths: Supporting Students Living with Trauma, Violence, and Chronic Stress* by Debbie Zacarian, Lourdes Alvarez-Ortiz, and Judie Haynes (#117035)

*Teaching with Empathy: How to Transform Your Practice by Understanding Your Learners* by Lisa Westman (#121027)

*Trauma Responsive Educational Practices: Helping Students Cope and Learn* by Micere Keels (#122015)

*Well-Being in Schools: Three Forces That Will Uplift Your Students in a Volatile World* by Andy Hargreaves and Dennis Shirley (#122025)

For up-to-date information about ASCD resources, go to **www.ascd.org**. You can search the complete archives of *Educational Leadership* at **www.ascd.org/el**.

**ASCD myTeachSource®**
Download resources from a professional learning platform with hundreds of research-based best practices and tools for your classroom at http://myteachsource.ascd.org/.

For more information, send an email to member@ascd.org; call 1-800-933-2723 or 703-578-9600; send a fax to 703-575-5400; or write to Information Services, ASCD, 2800 Shirlington Road, Suite 1001, Arlington, VA 22206 USA.

# WHOLE CHILD
# TENETS

### HEALTHY
Each student enters school healthy and learns about and practices a healthy lifestyle.

### SAFE
Each student learns in an environment that is physically and emotionally safe for students and adults.

### ENGAGED
Each student is actively engaged in learning and is connected to the school and broader community.

### SUPPORTED
Each student has access to personalized learning and is supported by qualified, caring adults.

### CHALLENGED
Each student is challenged academically and prepared for success in college or further study and for employment and participation in a global environment.

**ascd whole child**

The ASCD Whole Child approach is an effort to transition from a focus on narrowly defined academic achievement to one that promotes the long-term development and success of all children. Through this approach, ASCD supports educators, families, community members, and policymakers as they move from a vision about educating the whole child to sustainable, collaborative actions.

*From Stressed Out to Stress Wise* relates to the **healthy, safe,** and **supported** tenets.

*For more about the ASCD Whole Child approach, visit* **www.ascd.org/wholechild.**

**Become an ASCD member today!**
Go to www.ascd.org/joinascd
or call toll-free: 800-933-ASCD (2723)

**DON'T MISS A SINGLE ISSUE OF ASCD'S AWARD-WINNING MAGAZINE.**

If you belong to a Professional Learning Community, you may be looking for a way to get your fellow educators' minds around a complex topic. Why not delve into a relevant theme issue of *Educational Leadership*, the journal written by educators for educators?

Subscribe now, or purchase back issues of ASCD's flagship publication at **www.ascd.org/el**. Discounts on bulk purchases are available.

To see more details about these and other popular issues of *Educational Leadership*, visit **www.ascd.org/el/all**.

2800 Shirlington Road
Suite 1001
Arlington, VA 22206 USA

**www.ascd.org/learnmore**

www.ingramcontent.com/pod-product-compliance
Lightning Source LLC
Chambersburg PA
CBHW070733020526
44118CB00035B/1276